TOUGH PROBLEMS, REAL SOLUTIONS

Tough Problems, Real Solutions

A Q & A Book for Teens

JIM BURNS

SERVANT PUBLICATIONS
ANN ARBOR, MICHIGAN

Vine Books is an imprint of Servant Publications especia
evangelical Christians.

Servant Publications Mission Statement
We are dedicated to publishing books that spread the gospel of Jesus
Christ, help Christians to live in accordance with that gospel, promote
renewal in the church, and bear witness to Christian unity.

Published by Servant Publications
P.O. Box 8617
Ann Arbor, Michigan 48107
www.servantpub.com

Cover design: Uttley/DouPonce/Gilbert DesignWorks, Sisters, Oregon

02 03 04 05 10 9 8 7 6 5 4 3 2 1

Printed in the United States of America
ISBN 1-56955-347-5

Library of Congress Cataloging-in-Publication Data

Burns, Jim, 1953-
  Tough problems, real solutions : a Q & A book for teens / Jim Burns.
    p. cm.
Includes bibliographical references and index.
  ISBN 1-56955-347-5 (alk. paper)
  1. Teenagers–Religious life–Miscellanea. 2. Christian life–Miscellanea.
3. Teenagers–Conduct of life–Miscellanea. I. Title.
  BV4531.3 .B88 2002
  248.8'3–dc21

                                                    2002011792

Dedication

To Carrie Steele

You are one of the most dedicated coworkers I have ever known. Daily, you are an inspiration and embodiment of God's grace and love. Thank you for your presence in my life as coworker, assistant, representative, model of Christian living to my children, editor, "keeper of the gate" and God's precious gift to YouthBuilders and especially me.

Contents

Acknowledgments / 9

Topical Index / 11

ONE
Family / 15

TWO
Friends / 59

THREE
Self-Image / 77

FOUR
Teen Issues / 107

FIVE
Spiritual Life / 139

SIX
Church Life / 159

Thanks and Acknowledgments

A very special thanks to the thousands of *Campus Life* readers through the years who have written to me and shared their lives. I am a man most blessed and enriched by my relationship with you.

Thank you to Ruth Senter (my first editor at *Campus Life*) for inviting me to take on the Good Advice Column and cheering me on. A heartfelt thanks to Chris Lutes, Carla Barnhill and so many others at *Campus Life* who throughout the years have put out the finest Christian youth magazine in the world and cared deeply for kids and families. It is an absolute privilege to work with you.

Thank you to our wonderful staff at YouthBuilders. You are making a difference with your sacrifice of love and hard work.

Thank you to Jill Corey for all your help in the early days of the *Campus Life* column. Your fingerprints are all over this project and at YouthBuilders.

Lastly, I thank my own teenagers, Christy, Rebecca and Heidi. You have given me the vision to keep impacting teens and their parents as well as the knowledge that this is a most wonderful generation who will continue to make a positive impact on our world.

Topical Index

Abortion: 37
Abuse: 23, 25, 65
Accountability: 26, 29, 36, 38, 67, 76, 90
Adoption: 24
Anger: 5, 11, 13, 15, 18, 25, 34, 40, 47, 49, 61, 62, 65, 88, 91
Anxiety: 7, 10, 43, 44, 46, 48, 51, 52, 56, 69, 75, 85, 90
Alateen: 12
Al-Anon: 12

Baptism: 80
Bible Study: 13, 60, 76, 86, 93, 99, 101

Church: 20, 75, 80, 81, 83, 87, 91, 92, 93
Counseling: 5, 6, 8, 9, 13, 18, 23, 26, 39, 41, 42, 45, 59, 60, 67
Crime/Stealing: 68

Dating: 16
Dancing: 101
Death: 5, 15, 16, 34, 59, 60, 61, 99
Defiance: 3, 13, 18, 25, 31, 76, 88, 100
Depression: 9, 15, 40, 43, 44, 45, 46, 47, 49, 51, 52, 53, 59, 61, 62, 76
Disagreements: 1, 2, 6, 7, 9, 10, 20, 22, 100
Discipline: 1, 21, 67, 73, 81
Divorce: 7, 8, 10, 26
Drugs & Alcohol:
  Using: 31, 37, 57

Abusing: 58
Addiction: 12, 58

Eating Disorders: 11, 40, 42
Anorexia: 52
Bulimia: 41
Education: 81

Forgiveness: 98
Friends: 13, 28, 30, 31, 32, 33, 34, 35, 36, 37, 38, 50, 54, 55, 57, 58, 59, 61, 64, 68, 69, 70, 75, 88, 92

Gossip: 33, 35, 38, 54
Guilt: 7, 8, 10, 11, 16, 42, 44, 47, 56, 62, 68

Holy Spirit: 95, 96
Homosexuality: 14, 66
Honesty/Dishonesty: 24, 35, 36, 46, 55, 57, 61, 80, 91

Independence: 1, 3, 36, 38

Jealousy: 33, 48, 88

Loneliness: 15, 16, 29, 33, 44, 45, 47, 51, 53, 60, 61

Marriage: 5, 6, 26
Maturity: 1, 3, 46, 48, 67
Missions: 83, 84
Movies: 2, 70
Music: 22, 51, 70

Occult/Cults: 64, 97, 102, 103

Parenting: 1, 10, 17, 23, 24
Peer Pressure: 31, 35, 37, 38, 43, 48, 53, 55, 63, 68, 70, 72, 73, 75, 78, 100, 103
Pornography: 27
Prayer Life: 7, 9, 20, 21, 32, 37, 57, 60, 74, 77, 82, 87, 89, 90, 93, 94
Pregnancy: 37
Prejudice: 13, 46, 61, 66

Relationships: 15, 17
　　With parents: 1, 2, 3, 4, 5, 6, 7, 8, 9, 10, 11, 12, 14, 16, 20, 21, 23, 26, 27, 45
　　With peers: 28, 30, 33, 53, 65, 66, 70, 87
　　With siblings: 9, 18, 22, 65
Role Model: 14, 17, 19, 20, 21, 28, 31, 32, 34, 35, 36, 64, 66, 67, 70, 73, 90, 93

Salvation: 19, 23, 79, 99
Sarcasm: 19, 33, 35, 43, 88, 91
School: 69, 71, 81, 85
Self-abuse: 62
Self-centered: 36
Self-control: 13, 19, 40, 42, 56, 62, 65, 67, 72, 73, 75, 103
Self-esteem: 24, 33, 38, 40, 42, 43, 44, 46, 47, 48, 49, 50, 51, 52, 53, 62, 65, 68, 79
Sex:
　　Promiscuity: 26, 37
　　Sexual abuse: 25, 52, 65
　　Sexual identity: 66

Siblings: 9, 13, 15, 18, 19, 22, 65
Sin: 72, 96, 98
Smoking: 55, 56
Spiritual Life: 14, 15, 17, 20, 21, 22, 34, 42, 46, 56, 64, 74, 75, 76, 77, 78, 79, 80, 81, 82, 86, 87, 92, 93, 95, 103
Stepparents: 8, 9
Stress: 58
Studying: 81
Suicide: 98
   Attempted: 41,
   Thoughts of: 15, 23, 49, 51, 59
Support group: 5, 7, 27, 32, 45, 90, 92
Swearing: 72, 73

Tattoos/Makeup: 63, 100
Trinity: 95
Trust: 1, 3, 14, 16, 32, 33, 38, 66, 68, 76

Verbal abuse: 5, 19, 23, 25, 39
Volunteering: 76, 83

Weight: 11, 39, 40, 41, 43, 47, 53
Withdrawal: 18, 34, 45, 91
Witnessing: 28, 30, 57, 71, 80, 84, 85

Youth culture: 63, 92, 101, 102, 103
Youth group: 29, 31, 32, 87, 88, 89, 90, 92, 93, 94

ONE

Family

1. My Mom Is Not Fair

My mom doesn't let me do anything. I'm seventeen years old and still can't go out with my friends without permission. Although I go to church and have not done drugs or anything too rebellious, I have no freedom. When I try talking to her, she thinks I'm being smart. I don't know what to do. Please help me.

You're not alone on this one. Most seventeen-year-olds with caring, Christian parents think Mom and Dad are a little too strict. In your parents' defense, since you haven't done drugs or been too rebellious, they probably did something right! But what worked before isn't working so well for you now. The fact is, you're at a pretty awkward stage in family relationships—a time when you're rapidly moving from dependence on your parents toward much more independence. And it's going to be tough for everyone involved.

Here's what I would do if I were you. I would make a "contract" with your parents. I would state very clearly my specific desires for more independence. Then I would write out how the contract rules would change depending on whether or not I held up my end of the bargain.

For example, maybe your curfew is 10 P.M. and you want it

to be 11. Write on the contract that you would like your parents to move the curfew to 10:30 for a specific period of time—say the next three months. If you consistently make it home on time, then after three months your parents move the curfew to 11. If you fail to keep the new curfew, they move it back to 10 for three more months. That's the idea.

Here's what's great about the contract: Your actions, not your parents' rules, determine whether you are ready for more freedom, since you'll live by your wise or unwise decisions. The success or blame rests with you. So talk to your parents about trying out this idea. It might be just what you need.

2. I Can't Watch PG-13 Movies

I wanted to go see a PG-13 movie with some friends, but my parents said no. They said what goes in my mind comes out in my actions. But they watch R-rated movies. If as Christians we're supposed to glorify God, why can they watch R-rated movies, but I can't watch PG-13 movies?

For Christians today, it's not an easy decision when it comes to films and their ratings. I'm sure you would agree that just because a film is rated PG-13, it doesn't mean it's Sunday school clean.

Should your parents as Christians ever watch an R-rated movie? That decision is between them and God. Sometimes parents can seem hypocritical in their ways, but usually they truly have a justification for the decisions they make. If I were you, in the least judgmental way possible, I would ask them how they make their viewing decisions as adults and as Christians. You may learn something, and in just a few years you will have to make those same decisions on your own.

One of the major parts of your mom and dad's job description as parents is to teach you to discern what types of influences are healthy and not healthy for you. Whether we like it or not, parents are in the "protection business." I'm glad your parents care enough to make a decision.

My family has a Scripture verse on our refrigerator that has helped us when in doubt: "Finally, brothers, whatever is true, whatever is noble, whatever is right, whatever is pure, whatever is lovely, whatever is admirable—if anything is excellent or praiseworthy—think about such things" (Phil 4:8). There is room for negotiation with your parents. But I encourage you to practice patience and respect when you do disagree with them. And try to learn something from their decisions. In a few years you'll be deciding what movies you watch ... and God should be included in those decisions.

3. Mom Won't Trust Me

I've lost my mom's trust because of something I did. Now she won't let me do anything. She acts like she's always mad at me and makes me do more stuff around the house than my brother and sister. How can I get my mom's trust back and get her to start treating me better?

It's not easy to win back a person's trust. Think of someone who has broken your trust. I'll bet it took a while before you were able to trust that person again. Still, I believe you can earn your mom's trust back in time.

The truth is, the only way to earn your mom's trust is to show her you're trustworthy. Jesus once told a parable where the master said to his trustworthy servants, "You have been faithful with a few things. I will put you in charge of many things" (Mt 25:23). Take small steps toward earning your mom's trust. If you tell her you'll be home at a certain time, then be home on time, or call before you're late and tell her when you'll be home. If she asks you to clean your room or to run an errand for her, do it without grumbling. Be honest about your actions and in almost all cases, parents will eventually give you their trust again. As a parent of teenagers, I'm convinced most parents desperately want to trust their kids. Sure we can be overprotective and kind of hyper about the little things, but in general, if you're trustworthy, we'll give you more freedom.

Here's a real practical idea: Create a written agreement with your mom. This means the two of you sit down and write out exactly what she wants from you and what you'll promise to do. Take cleaning your room, for example. Discuss your mom's expectations. If you think her requests are fair and reasonable, write them out on a piece of paper. If you feel like she's asking too much, calmly talk more about it until you reach an agreement, then write it down.

Once you've agreed to a set of expectations, talk about the consequences if you mess up. Maybe she'll limit your phone privileges, or you can't have friends over for a few days. These "consequences" will help you work at being more trustworthy. There can also be good consequences. If you keep your word and your room stays reasonably clean for a month, celebrate with a special activity for just you and your mom.

The written agreement may seem kind of formal, but, believe me, it can work. Keep showing your mom you want things to get better between you, and I think you'll eventually regain her trust.

4. Mom's Too Busy for Me!

I need my mom as a friend. I can't tell her anything because she doesn't have time for me. I want to be closer to her, but I don't know how. Any advice?

Talk with your mom and tell her how you feel. Try not to make her feel guilty, but instead focus on how you're feeling. Don't shame her into spending time with you, but tell her specifically what you need or want from her. If she's too busy to sit down with you, write her a note. Say something like, "Mom, I love you and I really want to spend some time with you. I know you're busy, but I would like to invite you to go out to breakfast with me this Saturday."

Use this time to talk about your relationship. Your mom can be very special to you during your teenage years, but she *can't* or *shouldn't* always be just a friend to you. Sometimes the role of a mom is to show guidance, establish boundaries and provide discipline. However, she most likely desires the same special relationship that you do.

You really do need your mom's relationship. There may be no one besides God who is more important to your growth through the teenage years than your mom. Take the initiative and make it happen. Your mom will thank you for reminding her of her most important calling from God—to be your mom.

5. My Family's Falling Apart

My dad has never been the same since his father, mother and brother died over ten years ago. His temper became worse, he's verbally abusive, and now my mom says she doesn't love him anymore. She's going through changes of her own, drastic emotional ups and downs. I'm very scared and need help. What can I do?

What you can't do is solve your parents' problems. Both of them are dealing with issues that are beyond your control. The problem is that their issues are also affecting you. I would encourage you to find the support you need from outside your family. Is there someone, possibly even a group of people, from your church who can come alongside you? Don't wait for people to come to you; find people who can support you through these difficult times.

Although times are difficult right now, try not to be too discouraged. The good news in the midst of your parents' problems is that others have gone through these kinds of crummy situations and many have received the help needed to handle their pain in a positive manner. This doesn't mean your problems—or your parents' problems—will go away, but with the right kind of support you can make it through this season of your life and not have the same problems your parents have in their marriage.

I know one high school friend who had a very similar situation as you. She went to her pastor and got the support she needed to stay strong through her parents' problems. As her parents watched their daughter gain strength from God and the church, they also decided to seek help from the pastor. Today the entire family is in church leadership and doing well. Pray for your parents and get the help you need.

6. My Parents Hate Each Other

I'm eighteen, and my parents have a terrible relationship. Their hatred of each other is wearing on me physically and spiritually. My mother is a Christian and my father is Muslim, so I can't get them to see eye-to-eye on things like forgiveness. He has never physically abused any of us, but he flies into rages where he throws and hits things and screams profanities. What should my mother and I do?

You're in a difficult situation. And you're right; hate, rage and lack of forgiveness really do take a toll on us physically and spiritually. I urge you and your mom to seek wise counsel from a Christian family counselor in your area.

It seems like you're siding with your mom in these conflicts. While I understand that, I'd try to stay clear of their conflicts—unless you feel your mother is in physical danger.

You both need a support system to help change behavior patterns in the family. You may be able to find the help you need in your church. Your dad might also benefit from the loving, forgiving setting of the Christian church.

Even if your parents won't seek help, I urge you to find

someone you can confide in. Find someone who can help you avoid repeating your parents' mistakes, to stop the cycle of dysfunction from passing on to the next generation. And work hard to live a life that honors God.

I know a woman who came from a family much like yours. She was eighteen when she went to a Christian university, where she saw another way to live and decided she wouldn't imitate her parents' behaviors. Today she is happily married to a Christian youth worker, and their kids don't have to cope with all the problems she dealt with as a child. My friend decided to give her life wholeheartedly to God and work hard to overcome her childhood scars. You have the same opportunity. It will take a great deal of effort, but it will be worth it.

Finally, never give up praying for your parents. God is a God of miracles.

7. My Parents Are Splitting Up

My parents are about to split up and I'm scared. I've read about kids who get really messed up by their parents' divorce. How can I stay sane in the middle of my parents' fighting?

You are in for a ride on an emotional roller coaster. You've probably already been feeling all sorts of conflicting emotions: anger, fear, resentment, relief, sadness, guilt. And all of those are understandable responses to what's happening to you. But the last one, guilt, is one I hope you'll let go of. Here's why.

Guilt is a very common feeling among the children of divorcing parents. But you need to know that your parents' problems are not your fault. You didn't cause the potential divorce, and your parents might have had problems in their marriage long before you were born. Contrary to messages you might hear, you must believe that you are not to blame for your family's situation.

I'd advise you to find some supportive people you can talk to about your feelings and the stress of home. Your own parents are probably too emotionally drained to offer you much support right now. So find another adult friend, like your youth leader, who would be willing to talk with you on a regular basis. Your youth leader might even be able to point you to other students in your church who've gone through divorce and know how you're feeling.

You need supportive people you can trust—people who will listen to you, pray for you and sometimes just give you a hug. You can't magically take away your parents' problems, but you can build a foundation of strength in your life in order to handle your parents' divorce.

And, please, do not give up praying for your parents. They need God's comfort and his intervention. God is all for the reconciliation of marriages. Marriage is part of his plan for the family. In fact, I've seen the worst marriages brought back through prayer and spiritual intervention. If your parents do get divorced, life will definitely be different. However, large numbers of young people are affected by divorce, and many of them are making wise, godly decisions about their lives. You can too!

8. Dealing With Divorce

My parents recently got divorced. Since the divorce they've each found someone new. They want me to be happy for them and to accept the new people in their lives. I'm not trying to hurt my parents, but I find it difficult to even carry on a conversation with these people because I feel like I'm betraying my other parent. Please help.

One of the most common reactions of kids dealing with divorce is feeling torn between Mom and Dad. When this happens, it's important to remember your parents made the decision to separate, you didn't. Unfortunately that doesn't stop divorce from affecting you. In fact, one consequence is that there may eventually be someone else in the picture. You're in a difficult situation, but I don't think you're betraying either parent by having a conversation with the "other person."

I suggest talking to your parents about your feelings. (If you need to organize your thoughts, write them down first.) Tell your parents you love them. Then tell them you have a hard time talking with their newfound loves because you feel like you're betraying the other parent when you do. Ask them to be patient and understanding as you're also trying to work through the divorce.

In addition to going to God for strength and encouragement, you might also consider seeing a professional Christian counselor to help you sort out your feelings. Talking through your feelings and dealing with your emotions is the first step toward maintaining healthy relationships. More importantly, it will help you begin to heal.

9. Surviving a Stepfamily

My parents are divorced and my mom remarried a few years ago. But I don't get along with my new family. My stepsister is a real snob and totally rude. My mom and my stepdad argue all the time. I liked it so much better when it was just my mom, my brothers and me. I feel so depressed about this. What can I do?

Dealing with a "blended family" isn't easy, is it? But I do want to offer a few suggestions—and some hope.

There's a saying I use with my own teenage daughters. And I recently heard my oldest use it with one of her friends. It says, "Your circumstances may never change, but your attitude can change and that makes all the difference in the world." In other words, our attitudes can transcend our circumstances. You can't do much about your mom's choices. You also can't do much to change your stepsister's attitude. But you are in charge of *your* choices and attitudes. And your choices and attitudes will be your best tools in dealing with a tough situation.

Most blended families go through difficult times of adjustment. Perhaps the best thing you can do is lower your expectations. Whether you like it or not, your family isn't just you, your mom and your brothers anymore.

Your high expectations may also be the reason you're depressed. You may be feeling a deep sense of loss—your old life is gone and you're struggling to accept the reality of your new one. Allow yourself some time to adjust to things the way they are; that may be the first step to getting out of your depression. If you can't shake your depression in a few months, please seek Christian counseling. A counselor can help you find some ways to deal with your situation.

Rethinking your expectations won't be easy. But there are a few things you can do to get started. First, look carefully at your mom and stepdad's relationship. Do they really fight constantly, or does it just feel that way? And keep in mind that they're struggling with adjustments of their own, as well as trying to help their children settle in to this new family. Although you aren't responsible for what goes on between them, you can help ease the tension of the household by showing and telling each of them you care about them. Seeing you make an effort may help them do the same. Even if they continue to fight, you'll know you're doing your best to make your home a peaceful one.

You also need to have realistic expectations of your stepsister. You don't have to be best friends, but you do have to live in the same house. So do all you can to be pleasant and civil toward her. You may discover that her rudeness is just her way of dealing with the same kind of feelings you're experiencing.

Finally, make sure you have some strong Christians who'll talk and pray with you. I hope you're involved in the youth group at your church or a Christian club at school. The support of friends is essential. I also hope you have other adults in your life, like a youth pastor, whom you trust. Talk to them and seek their wisdom and encouragement.

One of my best friends grew up in a household very similar to yours. Like you, he felt depressed and struggled to be content with his new life. Eventually, he decided to accept what he couldn't change and to change what he had control over—himself. His problems didn't magically disappear, but by changing some of his expectations, and seeking the help of friends, he learned to make the best of things. His wise decisions, combined with God's help, have brought him a pretty good life. That's my hope for you, too.

10. I Want a Relationship With My Dad

My parents are divorced, and I hardly see my dad. I really love him and want to have a good relationship with him. But every time I try to talk to him about my feelings, he tells me they're wrong and I end up in tears. How can I talk to my dad and start improving our relationship?

Your desire to grow closer to your dad shows a lot of maturity. It would be easy for you to become angry with him, or blame him for the distance between you. Instead, you're choosing the harder, but more rewarding route of repairing a damaged relationship.

To start on those repairs, you definitely need to let him know how you're feeling. But since talking to him is so hard for you, you might want to write him a letter. Keep it honest and straightforward. Tell him how much you love him, and that you want to feel close to him. Be careful not to lay any guilt on him, or blame him. Just be honest about your own feelings.

Then make a specific request of him, like, "Dad, would you be willing to go out to lunch with me every Saturday?" If he lives far away, set up a weekly phone call. Once you find a time to talk, stick to it, no matter what. Show him your commitment to this relationship. Then start building from there. Get to know your dad. Find out how his week went. Ask about his job, his friends, his hobbies. And tell him about your week, your friends, your hobbies. For the first few weeks, avoid talking about your negative feelings. As you get more comfortable with your dad, it may become easier to talk about those feelings without the tears and frustration you feel now.

My guess is that your dad wants to have a better relationship, too. He may be as stumped as you are on how to begin. He may feel some guilt and shame over the divorce. Because he doesn't see much of you, he may feel like he doesn't know you very well. Or he may not be sure what it is you want from him. But as he gets to know you better, and gets the hang of talking about life with you, he may come around.

For now, I think you're going to have to do a lot of the work of improving things with your dad. But a good relationship is always worth the effort.

11. My Dad Is Obese

I try hard to love my dad, but he's obese, and I find myself getting angry at him for letting himself get like this. When I'm in a room with him, I often leave because I can't stand to be around him. I feel so awful, but I don't know what to do. Please help me out.

From the intensity of your letter, I wouldn't be surprised if, deep down inside, you do love your dad. Yes, you resent his obesity, and you're incredibly angry with him. But I want to challenge you to think about your feelings in another way. The fact is, love is probably causing you to feel anger toward your dad. You don't like his obesity because you're concerned about his health and self-image—because you want him to care more about himself, and about you. You love him, but you don't like his physical condition.

I have a friend whose mom was obese. The advice I gave him is the same advice I would give you. I suggested that he ask his mom to take a walk with him every day. He could get his mom out for a bit of exercise and at the same time build a positive relationship with casual conversation.

Here's what happened: As they walked, his mom began to open up about feeling terrible about her weight. My friend encouraged his mom to keep exercising and eat healthier meals. But he didn't stop there. He committed to doing this with her. Together, they set a workable goal to eat right and exercise daily. They kept each other accountable and rewarded themselves after a month of exercise and better eating.

Following this plan produced some great results for both my friend and his mom. First, my friend and his mom had better communication on those walks. He saw a sensitive side to her that he rarely experienced. Second, his mom lost some weight and began to feel better about herself. Later she found out she had an eating disorder called "compulsive eating." She would eat when she was depressed, which was almost all the time. Third, my friend shed a few excess pounds himself.

I hope you will follow my friend's actions and love your dad toward health. You may be surprised at how willing he is to respond to your love. And one last thing: Don't forget to pray daily for your dad. His obesity is probably either a true hormonal imbalance or a deep emotional, psychological and spiritual problem. He needs your love and your prayers.

12. My Dad's an Alcoholic

Until about a year and a half ago, I lived with my mom. Now I'm living with my dad, whom I haven't lived with in ten years. He's an alcoholic, and he doesn't like my Christian beliefs. He'll call home when he's drunk and swear and insult me. He's consumed with his job, his girlfriend and alcohol. I dread seeing him. But I really want a close relationship with him—isn't that what God would want? What can I do?

You've already done something significant by acknowledging that your dad is an alcoholic. He's addicted to a mood- and mindaltering drug, and you suffer the consequences of that addiction.

As you well know, living with an alcoholic isn't easy. I know, too—I grew up with alcoholism in my family. But it might help you to know that your dad probably doesn't like living with himself, either. He knows his alcoholism is partly to blame for some of the severe problems your family faces. Quite possibly he's tried to quit drinking at one time or another, but because of his intense addiction, and because alcohol effectively medicates his pain and relieves stress, he's been unsuccessful.

Let me give you four pieces of advice. First, begin meeting with someone who knows about being the child of an alcoholic. You can receive needed information and support from others who have struggled with the same situation. Your youth leader or school counselor can help you find this vital help. I would also recommend looking for Alateen and Al-Anon support groups (call 888-425-2666 or visit www.al-anon-alateen.org for a local chapter).

Second, continue communicating with your dad. Once you start receiving outside support, you'll gain more confidence to talk with your dad about your desire for a meaningful, deeper relationship. Tell your dad you love him. But remember: Most alcoholics have a difficult time with intimacy. You might have to lower your expectations of a "perfect" home and relationship. As you seek a healthier relationship, don't be afraid to call your dad's problem by name. He's an alcoholic; tell him you believe he can get help for his alcoholism. You can even help him find a local chapter of Alcoholics Anonymous by visiting www.alcoholics-anonymous.org.

Third, don't neglect yourself and your own needs. There is always the temptation to feel like you're responsible for somehow "fixing" your dad. You're not. You are responsible for taking care of yourself, so be sure you do. Build good friendships. Get exercise. Eat healthy. Find ways to relax and simply enjoy life. And be sure you stay away from alcohol and other substances. As strange as it sounds, children of alcoholics often turn to alcohol or other drugs to solve their problems. Don't give in to the temptation.

Finally, don't neglect your spiritual life. I like these verses: "You, Lord, give true peace to those who depend on you, because they trust you. So, trust the Lord always, because he is our Rock forever" (Is 26:3-4, NCV). God doesn't promise us an easy life, but he does promise to walk with us through our times of trouble.

As a Christian growing up in a family crippled by alcoholism, I felt at times like my faith was misunderstood. I wanted the kind of relationship with my parents that you want with your dad. And to be honest, I eventually gave up much hope in the situation ever changing. The fervent prayers I prayed in high school became less regular.

But God did get ahold of my family. It wasn't while I was still in high school, but today we have the relationship I always longed for. Keep praying for your dad, and don't give up hope.

13. He Deserves Worse Than Hell

My sister's ex-boyfriend abused her in every way you can think of. I don't ever want him to become a Christian. If he does, God is going to let him off the hook for all the awful things he did to my sister and is still doing to other girls. Even if he never becomes a Christian and goes to hell, it won't be enough punishment. I have so much anger in my heart because of this. I just want justice.

I felt your anger sizzle in your every word. And your anger is certainly understandable. It sounds like your sister was put through a lot. It is such a tragedy when good people are hurt by messed-up people. And I see by your desire for justice that you really love and care for your sister.

I believe you have good reasons to be angry. But remember, the Bible says, "in your anger do not sin" (Eph 4:26). Some people get so angry over terrible circumstances that they allow their anger to take over their life. At that point they are no longer ruled by love but trapped by a storm of resentment, animosity, hostility and rage. In a sense you are going through what some people call "the stages of grief." The anger stage of grief is the strongest and most intense.

The best way to deal with your anger is to continue to get your feelings out. In prayer, tell God how mad you are at this person who abused your sister. Speak with a counselor, pastor or concerned listener who will let you blow off some of the steam. This won't take the abuse away, but it will help you get through your intense anger.

You've said that no amount of punishment could be enough to compensate for the hurt done to your sister and others. Make sure you don't try to replace God on this issue. Believe it or not, he's more concerned about your sister's pain than you are, because he loves your sister even more than you do. And as crazy as it seems, he also loves her abuser. This guy's eternal life rests in the hands of God and no one else. We have to let God be God.

You and I do not have the capacity to comprehend all things eternal and spiritual. But we can be sure that if God is in charge of the universe, he's definitely in charge of this situation. When I am feeling like you are about a major injustice, I find this psalm of David to be very helpful and assuring:

"The Lord reigns forever; he has established his throne for judgment. He will judge the world in righteousness; he will govern the peoples with justice. The Lord is a refuge for the oppressed, a stronghold in times of trouble. Those who know your name will trust in you, for you, Lord, have never forsaken those who seek you" (Ps 9:7-10).

14. My Mom Is a Lesbian

My mom is a lesbian. I know that the Bible says it is wrong, but my mom says she falls in love with a person because of who they are inside. So my mom feels like it's OK if the person she loves is a woman. Why would God condemn my mom when she's trying to love

people for who they are? I really worry she is going to go to hell. Can you help me understand this?

Let me start by clearly saying this: God loves your mom. God allowed his only son, Jesus, to die for all people—including your mom.

Homosexuality is a very complicated and disturbing sin to many people, partially because they can't understand it. That may explain why some people act and talk as though homosexuality is a worse sin than others. Some people may not like what I'm going to say, but I don't think your mother's sin of homosexuality is any worse than the guy I know from my church who committed adultery, or the teenage girl who lies to her parents. In fact, there are references to all kinds of sin throughout the Bible, and only a few relate directly to homosexuality.

In Greek, the original language of the New Testament, the word "sin" literally means "to miss the mark." You don't get any extra points for only missing by a few inches. And you don't rack up penalty points for missing by a mile. You either hit the mark or you don't. And we all miss the mark—I do, you do, and your mom does.

I also believe the Bible is the Word of God, and I do believe the Bible clearly states that homosexuality is a sin. Your mom might disagree with me, but I have to stand by the authority of Scripture.

Still, my main concern right now is not so much your mom's sexual preference as her relationship with Jesus Christ. If she truly gives her life to Christ, confesses her sin (not just sexual sin, but all sin) and accepts his death on the cross as

God's ultimate act of forgiveness, then she will be saved. Romans 10:9-10 says, "If you confess with your mouth, 'Jesus is Lord,' and believe in your heart that God raised him from the dead, you will be saved. For it is with your heart that you believe and are justified, and it is with your mouth that you confess and are saved." It doesn't matter if you're a homosexual, a liar, a cheat or any other kind of sinner; the way to salvation is the same for everyone.

If someone does make a sincere profession of faith in Christ according to Romans 10:9-10, they will want to make Jesus the Lord of their life, and they will look to the authority of the Bible for guidance. They will desire to live a life free from sin. They will strive to glorify God in all they say and do. For some people, that might mean they give up a way of life based on greed and deceit. For others, it might mean they no longer lie or gossip about others. For a homosexual, it means seeking a lifestyle that is consistent with the Bible's views on sexuality. Of course, no one can ever live completely free from sin, but following Christ means we do everything in our power to honor God with the way we live.

I think it's safe to say God is less concerned with the specific sin in a person's life than with the way sin affects that person. God wants to have a relationship with us, and sin gets in the way. Sin hurts us and makes our lives less than what God wants them to be. If your mom is like most homosexuals, I doubt she has lived an easy life. Studies tell us that homosexuals as a group are less happy, less fulfilled, more involved in drug and alcohol abuse, and frankly, often die much earlier than heterosexuals.

So is your mom condemned to hell? I honestly can't answer

that question. Ultimately, that's between her and God. If she gives her life to Christ and truly seeks to live for him, then the Bible promises she'll spend eternity in heaven. God really does want to know her and see her in heaven one day (see 2 Pt 3:9). It's up to her to make the choice.

I encourage you to pray for your mom. When you have questions or concerns about your mom's homosexuality, talk to a trustworthy adult from your church. Continue to show your mom love and respect, and let her know you care about her, no matter what.

15. I Can't Get Over My Mom's Death

My mom died a year ago and I'm still having a really hard time with it. I've talked to my youth pastor and written poems about my feelings, but nothing seems to help. I'm so depressed. I've thought about killing myself, but I know that would just make things worse for my family. I'm not close to my dad or my brother or sister, so I really can't talk to them about how I feel. It just hurts so much. What can I do?

There's nothing worse than the sting of death. The extreme loss and pain you're feeling is very normal. Losing a parent at a young age is a horrible ordeal. Nothing I can say can take away your pain, but maybe I can help you understand what's going on.

You're experiencing grief. Anyone who has been through a situation like yours has experienced grief and yet each person deals with grief differently. Your brother and sister, even your dad, are all handling their pain in a different manner than you. So far you've made some very wise decisions in the midst of your pain. You've met with your youth pastor. That's a great idea. If your youth pastor is a good listener, keep on talking to him or her. If you feel like you need more help, please don't hesitate to go to a Christian counselor. There are actually people who specialize in grief counseling. Your youth pastor can probably help you find this kind of counselor. If not, contact an area hospital and ask about grief counseling.

You've also done a good thing by writing poems about your feelings. During times of deep sadness and grief it is important to get our feelings out as much as possible. Even if the feelings don't make much sense or are buried deep inside, writing can help bring them to the surface where you can deal with them. People who deal with their feelings head-on (like you) usually feel their pain more intensely, but they end up working through their grief in a healthier, more effective way than those who ignore their feelings of loss.

You mentioned that you've actually thought of suicide. Again, this is a pretty normal reaction to extreme emotional pain. And you sound like you're handling your depression and even feelings of suicide in a healthy manner. Intellectually, you have decided that obviously, suicide is the wrong decision. But if you ever go further than just thinking about it and you actually plan a time, method or place for killing yourself, or you begin to feel out of control of your life, please talk to someone immediately.

Even though you don't feel close to your dad or your brother or sister, I'd suggest you keep the communication lines open. They may not be your primary source of comfort or the only people you share your feelings with, but they are your family. As you go through this tragedy together, you need to be able to talk with each other about your feelings. As you lean on each other and seek to understand each other's feelings, you'll naturally grow closer together.

Also, do all you can to stay close to God during this time of grief. If you have some anger and doubts, tell him. While he hasn't guaranteed our lives will be free from pain this side of heaven, he has clearly promised to walk with us even in the shadow of death (see Ps 23). Because he loves you and knows you so well, he understands your pain like no one else can. Turn to him, and eventually you will find comfort.

16. Dad Wants to Date

Ever since my mom died, my dad's been really lonely. He wants to meet a nice woman and maybe go on some dates, but he's really shy. He asks my advice a lot, but I'm not sure what to tell him. See, I'm not sure I'm ready to see him with someone else. I know that's selfish. I really would like him to be happy again. I've talked to him about some of my feelings, but then I just feel bad for making things more difficult for him. How can I get over my selfish feelings and help my dad?

I don't think your feelings are selfish. I think they're normal. To lose your mom is incredibly difficult. And I can understand why it's difficult to think of your dad falling in love with someone new. So give yourself some time.

I'm glad you and your dad have a good relationship. I like

the fact that you've talked with him about your feelings, and I'm very impressed that your dad has shared his feelings of loneliness with you. It's clear you're close to your father and that you can share even difficult times together. It's also clear you care deeply about your father and want him to be happy. But I think you're at a different stage in the grieving process than your dad. Only time will help you accept the idea of him dating. My own mother died three years ago. My dad is now remarried and, believe me, as happy as I am for him, it's taken me awhile to accept the fact that he's got a new life with a new woman.

One suggestion I would give you is to talk about your feelings with someone besides your dad, such as your youth pastor or another trusted adult. I'm not saying you should hide your feelings from your dad. I just think it's a good idea to bring someone else into the picture who can offer another perspective.

When my friend Todd lost his wife to cancer, he needed several people to come alongside him and give him perspective. Todd actually thought about these people as the "team" he needed to help him through his pain and brokenness. Everyone on the team had a role to play. I was the friend who took him out to lunch on a regular basis. Sometimes we talked about intense issues. Other times we just laughed and remembered funny stories about his wife. Todd also knew he needed to talk to a professional grief counselor. And Todd spent time with his pastor, some golfing buddies and his parents.

If you haven't already, I'd suggest you and your dad each create "teams" of your own—people who will help you deal with your terrible loss. Those people can be peers and adults, friends and relatives. Whoever they are, they should be people you can trust to be there for you when you need them.

I wish both you and your father the best as you continue to deal with a very difficult situation.

17. Embarrassed to Be a Christian

My whole family is Christian, but you'd never know it. We never talk about our faith or do devotions together. I try to have my own devotions, but I close my Bible and put it away when I hear my mom coming. Why am I ashamed of my time with God? Why won't the rest of my family open up about their faith?

Unfortunately you're describing a pretty normal Christian family. It's my guess your family has a desire to grow spiritually together, but they just don't get around to it. The intent and desire are there, but the action isn't. Maybe your family just needs someone to take the initiative to get them going. And it might as well be you.

Here's an idea. Talk with your youth worker or visit www.YouthBuilders.com to get family devotional material. Then, ask your parents to schedule a quick family meeting. At that meeting, present the idea of getting together weekly for a short (fifteen minutes or less) family devotional time. Since you're the one taking this initial step, tell your family you'll take responsibility for planning the first couple of devotions.

Your time together doesn't have to be anything formal. You could include a Scripture passage, some time to talk about what you've read, and prayer. In our family, we sometimes write our prayer requests on a 3x5 index card, exchange cards with another family member, then pray for them during the week.

Having a regular time with God is about the wisest and most important decision you can make. I would think your family would be extremely proud of your desire to grow in your faith. That desire is nothing to be ashamed of. And it could very well be contagious.

18. My Brother Has Fallen Away From God

My dad's a pastor, but my brother says he doesn't believe in God anymore. My brother recently got married, and I was the only member of our family who was invited. I want my family to be close again, but my brother won't talk to anyone but me. What can I do?

You sound like a courageous person. I'm glad that, despite the tension in your family, you're committed to your brother and to keeping your family close.

Since I don't know the details of why or when your family's struggles started, I can only assume it has to do with your brother's rejection of your family's faith. Of course, most family problems arise from a number of factors, not just one event or disagreement. Hurt feelings and unresolved conflicts can build over the years and explode in the kind of family crisis you've described. The dynamics between family members are often so complicated, it can take years to unravel and understand them.

Still, I have some suggestions that might help you and your family.

Pray daily for reconciliation. God is the creator and the sustainer of families. I believe he cares more about the situation than even you do. He knows the pain you and the rest of your family are experiencing. Ask God to soften the hearts of your family. Ask for strength and patience for yourself as you struggle to bring your family together. Pray that God will bring healing and reconciliation. And ask God to use you as an example of his peace in the middle of a difficult situation.

Seek outside help. It would be wonderful if your whole family, your brother included, could find a Christian counselor who could help you work through this situation. It can't hurt to ask your family members if they are open to getting help. If they are, counseling could be the first big step toward restoring your family. But if they aren't, I still encourage you to talk about your feelings with a Christian counselor, your youth pastor or another caring adult. Sometimes pastors' kids feel weird about sharing the family's problems, so you may want to talk with someone who's not a part of your church family.

Show God's love. One of my favorite Scripture passages is 1 Corinthians 13:4-8. It says, "Love is patient, love is kind. It does not envy, it does not boast, it is not proud. It is not rude, it is not self-seeking, it is not easily angered, it keeps no record of wrongs. Love does not delight in evil but rejoices with the truth. It always protects, always trusts, always hopes, always perseveres. Love never fails." When you're not sure how to deal with your parents or your brother, remember that love is the ultimate guide.

Finally, I hope you'll continue to show love and respect to your brother and the rest of your family. And don't give up on God's power to change the situation. If God's love was part of your brother's childhood, and your family has built a solid Christian foundation, there's a good possibility that one day your brother will be drawn back to the positive power of his roots in Christ.

19. My Brother-in-Law Is Not a Christian

My older sister recently married a guy I don't get along with. He's not a Christian, and he's blatantly disrespectful of my family's Christianity. I'm especially concerned that he will influence my sister and she'll lose her faith. I'm afraid to stand up to him, because I don't want to cause problems in the family. I don't know what to do.

I want to make a challenging suggestion to you. Try to win your new brother-in-law over by loving and serving him. Grab your Bible and read John 13:1-17. In this incredible scene, Jesus teaches us that following Christ means serving others. Jesus, the Son of God, humbled himself and washed his disciples' feet, showing them he was not only their teacher and Lord, but their servant too. He then tells them to follow his example and serve each other.

I'm not suggesting you wash your brother-in-law's toes, but I believe the way to a nonbeliever's heart is through a consistent, loving and serving attitude toward them. So start looking for ways to show God's love to your sister and brother-in-law. Run an errand for them; make them a nice meal. And occasionally ask your brother-in-law about hobbies, sports or other things he's interested in. When you ask, be sure to listen to what he has to say. Your interest in him and his life will show him you care about him as a member of your family.

Let's face it, your sister chose to marry this guy. Maybe no one else in your family would have voted him to be your sister's husband, but what's done is done. It's true your sister's faith may slip because of her husband's influence, but keep in mind what Jesus said in the Sermon on the Mount: "Let your light shine before men, that they may see your good deeds and praise your Father in heaven" (Mt 5:16). If you keep the positive light of God surrounding your sister and her husband, I believe they'll eventually be drawn to the source of that light.

20. I'm a Christian, My Family Is Jewish

I just became a Christian. I know I'm now born again, but my family is Jewish. My family feels very strongly about their religion, and they can't seem to accept this change in me. I don't judge them because their beliefs are different from mine, but they judge me. How can I get them to be happy for me and understand what my faith means to me?

Your decision to make Jesus the Messiah of your life is a courageous decision. When the Jewish leader, Nicodemus, talked with Jesus about being "born again" (Jn 3:1-22), I imagine he not only had to struggle to understand the truth, but he also had to figure out how to deal with his family and the religion of his youth. Would he follow what he perceived to be the truth, or would he stick with the religion practiced by his family? The Bible doesn't tell us how Nicodemus handled his family, but we do know he continued to support Jesus' ministry (Jn 7:50-52) and even helped prepare Christ's body for burial (Jn 19:39).

I would strongly suggest that you immediately get in touch with other Jewish believers who claim Jesus as the Messiah. If you don't know anyone else, you can call Jews for Jesus at (415) 864-2600 or check out www.jewsforjesus.org. They can help you find other Jewish believers in your area and perhaps give you some excellent counsel.

In the meantime, don't expect your family to be excited about your newfound faith in Jesus. They probably have some fears that you'll leave your roots. But you can reassure your family that since Christians also believe in the Old Testament, your new faith has a great deal in common with your family's faith.

You don't need to reject any of the Jewish customs or celebrations from the Old Testament. In fact, because so much of the Old Testament points to Jesus, you will probably understand many of the Jewish celebrations better than you did before. When your family sees you still participating in the Jewish celebrations and many of the rituals, some of their fears might be relieved. You can even attend synagogue with your family on Saturdays, then attend a church on Sundays. Make sure you let them know that you are not ignoring or disowning your Jewish heritage.

As a new Christian, you will want to grow in your faith. I hope you'll commit to reading the Bible daily, praying often, meeting with other believers regularly and serving God. One of the key points of Judaism is the covenant God created with Israel. And as you spend more time in the New Testament, you will see how the beauty and richness of the Old Testament mixes so wonderfully with God's "new covenant," the covenant of Christ.

21. Who Do I Obey, God or My Parents?

I'm the only Christian in my family. I pray for them, but I'm afraid they won't go to heaven unless they accept Jesus into their lives. The problem is, my parents forbid me to talk to them about God. If I obey God, who says we should spread the gospel, I will be disobeying my parents. If I obey my parents, I'm disobeying God. Who should I obey, God or my parents?

Your situation isn't an easy one, but I think you can obey both God and your parents. First and foremost, continue to pray for your family. God loves them and wants them to follow him even more than you do. And continue to obey your family. You don't have to talk about God to show your faith to your family. Your Christian lifestyle of love will say more to them than any words could ever do. As St. Francis of Assisi said, "Preach the gospel! And if necessary use words."

I also grew up in a family that wasn't very enthusiastic about my faith in Jesus Christ. One day during my college years, I was sitting in a chapel service and the speaker stood up to give his message. He didn't start with a Scripture, a funny story or even a greeting. He just said, "You are the only Jesus somebody knows." He then said it again, "You are the only Jesus somebody knows." This guy repeated that statement nine times and on the tenth time he pointed right at me and said those same words again. I don't remember another word he said that day. But it was as if God was speaking directly to me. The message was clear: I represented Jesus Christ to a family who did not know him. If they wanted to see what Jesus Christ was doing in the world, they were going to look at me.

You're right. Your family won't go to heaven unless they decide to put their faith in Jesus. But remember, they need to make the decision to follow Jesus on their own. Your responsibility is to simply live as much like Christ as you can.

You are God's representative to your family. Nowhere in the Bible does it say it will be easy. But God does promise to walk with you. Your job is to obey God and obey your family. Take a look at the Ten Commandments. God's will for our lives is spelled out clearly. In commandments one through four, God tells us to love and honor him. The fifth commandment says, "Honor your father and your mother, so that you may live long in the land the Lord your God is giving you" (Ex 20:12).

By loving and obeying your parents, you are obeying God.

22. I Can't Get Along With My Brother

My brother is a year younger than I, and we fight all the time. We both go to church, and attend our youth group. But he's not interested in really living for Christ. He uses bad language and listens to a lot of raunchy music. We used to have a great brother/sister relationship, and I'd like to have that again. How can we get past our differences and learn to get along?

Restoring your relationship is going to take patience, under-standing and a lot of commitment on your part. With that in mind, there are a few things you need to consider.

First, think about other relationships in your life. I'll bet each of them has had ups and downs. Even best friends argue, disagree and think differently about important issues. But when you are committed to a friendship, you're willing to work through those differences and repair the friendship. The same is true in your relationship with your brother. So don't let yourself get too worried that the way things are right now is the way they will be forever.

Also, realize your brother may be going through a rebel-lious stage in his life. But no matter how he acts on the out-side, he most likely still needs to feel loved and cared for. By sticking by him and continuing to show him you care, you'll send an invaluable message to your brother—one that says your love is permanent and unconditional.

To show your brother that kind of love, you need to focus on what's right in your relationship. Think about some of the things you have in common. Do you both like sports? Is there a movie or TV show that always makes you two laugh? Anything that helps you stay connected with your brother can help get you through this tough time.

Even if you can't find any common interests, you can still connect with your brother by expressing interest in his life. Yes, he's listening to music you find offensive, but do your best not to judge your brother. If you really want to be close to him again, you won't get very far by criticizing him or pointing out all the ways he's messing up. Instead, continue to show your brother God's love through your patience and care.

Finally, watch out for your brother. His change in behavior may indicate other, more dangerous changes, like alcohol or drug use. You don't need to spy on him, but be aware of who he's hanging out with and what kind of things he's doing after school. If you become concerned about anything, talk to your parents or another trusted adult, like your youth pastor.

Most importantly, pray for your brother. Ask God to be with him and to guide his decisions. And ask for God's wisdom as you work to repair your relationship.

After all of this, remember that your brother may not respond the way you want him to. But be patient. Hopefully, he will move out of this phase. My guess is that he really does want to be close to you, too, but he may not know how.

I know a brother and sister who are very close. They are each married and have their own families now, but even their families are the best of friends. They told me it wasn't always this way. After I read your letter, I called them and asked their advice. I think their answer is worth repeating: "Even in the most difficult times, try not to do permanent damage to the relationship and don't give up. A brother/sister relationship is a lifelong relationship, and when your brother gets through this awkward stage he will again look to your relationship as a priority."

23. My Mom Hates Me

My mom yells at me and makes fun of me. I don't know what I did to deserve this, but I must have done something for her to be so mean to me. Sometimes she gets this look in her eyes that terrifies me. She's

hit me before and I'm afraid she'll hit me again. I feel like my only options are to run away or kill myself. I don't know what else to do.

Please don't hurt yourself. Remember, suicide is a permanent solution to a temporary problem. For some people, suicide seems like the easiest way to get rid of their deep pain. But when they truly look at the problems causing these intense feelings, there is always a better answer than suicide. The same is true for running away. The people I know who've run away usually come back to the same problems. Sometimes, they make choices of their own that lead to even worse problems than those they tried to escape. Neither option solves much of anything.

In your situation, it sounds like the best solution is for your mother to get professional counseling. There must be an incredible amount of pain in her life that's causing her to be so harsh with you. Obviously, all families have their moments of shouting or bickering, but if you and your mom are unable to communicate in ways that don't involve yelling, insults and hitting, there is a definite problem.

If your mother is unwilling to get help, the best you can do is take steps on your own to help your family. As difficult as that sounds, I believe your letter is a good indication that you have the strength to do it. You don't mention your father. If he's still living with your family, and is someone you feel comfortable talking to, enlist his help in improving your relationship with your mother.

If he's not around, your first step should be to find a Christian adult you can trust, perhaps your pastor, a school counselor or a friend's parent. You need a supportive adult you can talk to and pray with regularly. It's important that you tell this person about your mom's behavior. You say she's hit you in the past. This physical abuse, as well as the emotional abuse you seem to be suffering, is wrong and needs to be dealt with by people trained to help abusive parents. An adult friend can help you find those people.

The next step is to get some professional counseling of your own. Ask your adult friend to help you find a Christian counselor who can help you deal with the heavy emotional toll this situation is having on you. Since your mother may be unwilling or unable to change, it's important that you learn new ways of relating to her.

Finally, I'd like to tell you about a person I know who had a problem similar to yours. She tried running away. She even attempted suicide. These choices only created more problems for her. One day, she decided there wasn't a whole lot she could do to change her mother, but there were several things she could do to face her own problems. She received some excellent Christian counseling and she joined a support group at her church. Although her problems didn't go away, she got great insight and communication tools from the counselor and received comfort and prayer from the support group. With help from these Christians who cared, she made it. I know you can make it, too.

24. I Was Adopted

I'm sixteen years old. When I was four, my parents told me I was adopted. I know God has placed me with my family for a special

reason, but I'm starting to wonder about my birth parents and my background. How can I talk to my parents about my questions without hurting their feelings?

I appreciate your sensitivity to your parents' feelings. Your desire to seek information on your background and birth parents is very normal. And even though it might be hard, I think you should talk with your parents about your questions. Here's why:

Before my wife and I were married, we would talk for hours about how many kids we wanted someday and what we would name them. After our wedding, we even discussed how long we wanted to wait until we became parents. After a few years of trying to have kids, we found out we were unable to bear children. We were devastated. It was the most difficult news we had ever received.

But the day we adopted our first child was one of the greatest days of my life. To this day, we are still grateful to our daughter's birth mother. By choosing adoption for her baby, she showed a depth of unconditional love that is almost unfathomable.

To be perfectly honest, I used to worry that the adoption would potentially cause our daughter and us some emotional pain. I knew that she would probably want to know more information about her birth mother and her background one day. But because I love my daughter so much, I want the best for her. So if and when she wants to know more information, I will help her understand her roots in any way I possibly can. If it is important to her, it's important to me.

As you discuss this issue with your parents, be sensitive to their potential fears. Some adoptive parents can become very insecure when the issue of seeking birth parents is brought up. We can be afraid of rejection or afraid that you're hurt by the adoption. So reassure your parents of your love for them. Continue to honor and respect them. Seek their advice as you work through your questions.

In most states, the law says you must be eighteen to search for your birth parents. If you decide you want to find your birth parents when you turn eighteen, ask your mom and dad for their blessing. They can be a great support to you as you try to learn more about this part of your life. Including your parents in your search for answers will help all of you remember that you will always be a very special family.

25. My Father Abused Me

I was sexually, physically and emotionally abused by my father when I was young. I've been in counseling for a long time, but I still can't stop being angry about this. I want to know where God was when I was being abused. Why didn't he make my dad stop? I grew up feeling hopeless and helpless and believing God didn't care about me. Now I can't trust God. I can't depend on him or turn to him for help. I begged for his help before and it never came. It isn't enough to hear God cares, or that he really was there, because I feel the effects of my abuse much more than I have ever felt God's help. I want to know why God let this happen to me.

I wish I could wave a magic wand and make all your pain and trauma go away. I wish you, and many others who talk with me, didn't have to go through the horrible abuse that took place in your lives. It seems like anything I write will sound trite compared to the immense pain in your life.

We're often left with more questions than answers in these tragic situations. I believe Jesus Christ can, and does, identify with you. As he hung on the cross in agony, I believe he felt your hopelessness and pain. He must have felt alone, abandoned and perhaps deeply hurt at the fact that he was innocent, yet had to be punished for the sins of the world. If Christ were with you in the flesh right now, I honestly think you would sense his love for you and his grief for what your father did to you. God is the loving, caring Father you didn't have on earth, and I believe he's hurt to the core by what happened to you.

I'm sure it's difficult for you to envision a Father who cares for you and loves you deeply, since your own father treated you so badly. And it may take many more years of healing before you're able to think of God as a loving Father. But I want to encourage you to look for ways God is showing you his love right now. You may even want to read what the Bible has to say about God's tremendous love for you. Here are just a few verses you could look at: Jeremiah 31:3-5; Romans 8:15-17; 1 John 4:9-10. I hope these verses will help you see the loving God who cares about what has happened to you.

You ask a difficult question: Why didn't God stop the abuse? I wish I knew what to tell you. Perhaps that can be your first question to God when you reach heaven. I honestly think when you are with God in eternity, you'll understand what happened and you won't blame him anymore. But I want to be very honest with you, I'm not sure anyone but God can answer your very important question.

My hope and prayer for you is that you will continue to get

help and that you won't turn away from God. Even though you and I don't have all the answers, this life is a snap of the fingers compared to eternity. I believe God never breaks his promises. God didn't promise us lives without pain here on earth, but he did promise us an eternal life with no tears or sorrow.

I hope that in the midst of your pain, you'll see glimpses of God's love for you now and in the glorious life to come.

26. My Mom's Flirting Online

My parents' marriage hasn't been going well for a while. And now my mom has been talking online with a male friend she met a long time ago. When I approached her about it, she told me everything was innocent and I was crazy to think otherwise. But later I found some evidence that proves it isn't innocent. I don't know what to do.

You are in a very difficult situation. Some people would simply ignore the possible signs and others would confront their parent with the information. Both ways of dealing with the problem are complicated and can be messy for the relationship. Let me first say that you don't have to feel like you're the ultimate savior of your parents' marriage. It's not your fault they're having problems, and it's not your responsibility to make all their problems go away. Having said that, I'd suggest you lovingly confront your mother about the new evidence. It's her responsibility to react to what you say. She may do it with wisdom and maturity, or she may not. Your job, if this is the direction you choose to go, is to put the information in front of her and reassure her of your love. Encourage her to go to a pastor or a counselor for help.

Far too many people your age put themselves in the middle of what feels like a Ping-Pong game, being bounced back and forth with their parents' problems. With that said, I must encourage you not to try to handle this all on your own. Seek help, advice and support from an adult you trust. You may want to look to one of your youth workers as a source of strength. They'll never take the place of your parents, but they may give you some God-honoring counsel that at this point you aren't getting from your parents.

27. My Dad's Into On-Line Porn

I was using my dad's computer and looked at his Internet history files and found porn sites. I think this is disgusting. It's actually not the first time I've seen this type of stuff on his computer. I thought it had stopped, but I was wrong. What can I do besides pray for him?

It's frightening just how many men are jumping into the scary pit of Internet pornography. Your dad needs help, and most likely, if confronted, he will experience incredible shame. Experts tell us that the power of pornography to rule our minds is as intense as a drug or alcohol addiction.

The Bible is clear when it comes to immorality. "It is God's will that you should be sanctified: that you should avoid sexual immorality" (1 Thes 4:3). The word "sanctified" literally means "to be set apart" or holy. We are challenged to be different from the world.

It's important to point out that the New Testament Greek word "pornia" is translated as "immorality." This is the same root we find in the word "pornography." The Bible is clear: We must avoid any type of sexual immorality including the use of Internet pornography. Another Scripture tells us to "flee from sexual immorality" (1 Cor 6:18).

Your dad is probably hurting as he mixes the temptation of his sin with the desire to avoid pornography. So what should you do? I don't believe it's your role to help your dad work through his problem with porn. But since you've found the evidence, you should confront him—in love, not in anger—with what you've found. I'd suggest saying something like this, "Dad, I found more history of porn sites on your computer. I'm sure you don't want to keep going in that direction. Here are a couple of organizations who might be able to help." Suggest Pure Intimacy (www.pureintimacy.org), Sexaholics Anonymous (www.sa.org, 615-331-6230 or Sex Addicts Anonymous (www.sexaa.org). You might also encourage him to talk to a pastor or Christian counselor.

I think you also must express your love and prayers for him. If you continue to see evidence that he's still involved with pornography, talk with a counselor or pastor who could help you deal with the issue. In these kinds of situations, we can and must reach out to our loved ones, but they are the ones who must ultimately make the decision to change.

TWO

Friends

28. My Friends Don't Act Like Christians

Three of my friends at school claim to be Christians, but don't act like it. I don't think they really understand what it means to be a Christian. How do I tell them they're not acting like real Christians without preaching at them?

You need to know you aren't the only Christian with this problem. You can sure offer your friends advice and confront them in a gentle way, but your positive Christian lifestyle will probably impact them more.

Imagine for a moment a pyramid. At the base of the pyramid is the "come and see" level of commitment to God. These are people who may come to church to check out the youth group, but don't have a faith of their own. The next level of commitment is a "casual believer." This may be the level your friends are on. The next level of commitment is the "disciple." The disciple has a more mature faith. That's probably where you fit in. There aren't as many "disciples" as "casual believers" and not as many "casual believers" as "come and see" people.

Your job is to help your casual believing friends move up the pyramid to a more committed discipleship life. I think this happens as they get more involved with Bible study, personal devotions, serving others, sharing their faith and being in an accountability group with other Christians. Continue to be patient and slowly encourage these friends to get more involved. God is very patient with us, and we must be patient with our friends. Invite them to your youth group or Christian club so they can see some of those disciple-type Christians in action. Finally, pray for your friends, and look for opportunities to help them move up the pyramid of commitment.

29. I Need a True Friend

I have moved around a lot because of my parents' jobs, so I'm not in a youth group anymore. Right now it seems I have no one to lean on. I sometimes attend church, but don't have a true church home. I don't understand why God is letting this happen to me. Do you have any advice?

It is very important that you find "community." Community is a sense of belonging. We all need it. Very few people can thrive in their faith without community. Even though you move frequently, you can still try to find a close group of Christian friends.

Throughout Scripture, God tells his people to share fellowship with other believers. In the Old Testament the theme is often about being "connected" to a group of believers. The New Testament says we should not "give up meeting together, as some are in the habit of doing, but let us encourage one another—and all the more as you see the Day approaching" (Heb 10:25). The word picture from the mouth of Paul is that we are all important parts of the body of Christ who need each other very much. (Read 1 Corinthians 12.)

Let me challenge you to find a youth group and church that fits you. No group will be perfect, and it will take time to feel connected. In order to speed up the process—join a small group, attend a retreat or spend one-on-one time with a student leader or youth worker in the church.

When I was a youth pastor, Kristi, a girl in my group, had a similar problem because her parents moved often. The first day I met her she put out her hand, greeted me and said, "I've just moved to this area. I've been checking out youth groups and want to commit to this one. I will probably move in the next couple of years so I want to get involved right away." I was impressed with her attitude. Kristi jumped right in, and after a few months she really was a major part of our group. I'm sure our youth group wasn't exactly like her last one, but she put it behind her and got involved. I suggest you follow Kristi's example and find a sense of belonging with Christians in your area.

30. How Can I Help My Friend?

My best friend isn't a Christian. I know you're supposed to have Christian friends but I can't stop being friends with her. We do things together and we always have fun. But when I try to talk to her about God, she says she's just not ready to commit to him. I take her to church every Sunday. She says she has fun, but I just want to make sure she becomes a Christian. What should I do?

Being a Christian doesn't mean you have to give up all your non-Christian friends. Non-Christians are not terrible people. On the contrary, some of the most generous and loving people I know are not Christians. I learn from them, enjoy their company and am challenged by their questions. I encourage you to keep relationships with non-Christians because through your loving example, they may come to know Jesus.

But to be a growing believer, you also need friends who will challenge you spiritually. Make sure you're developing strong relationships with believers who can build you up in your faith. I must also caution you to be aware of your relationships with non-Christian friends. Be sure those friendships aren't leading you to do, say or think things that are contrary to your Christian values.

As for reaching out to your friend, it sounds like you're doing a fine job. You bring her to church, you pray for her, you share your life with her. You can also witness to your friend by doing a Bible study together. I suggest going through the Gospel of Mark and studying the life and teachings of Jesus. This way she'll gain a better understanding of who Jesus is.

Never forget that God cares more for your friend's soul than you do. Your job is to be faithful to your friend. God's job is to draw her to himself. What an awesome thought that he would use you to influence your friend for eternity!

31. Can He Be a Christian?

I've got a good friend who says he's a Christian, but he only acts like one at youth group. At school, he's always talking about drinking and

smoking pot. He knows I don't like drinking or drugs, and he resents me for telling him that. I've prayed for him a lot, but he just seems to be getting further and further into stuff he shouldn't. How can I help him?

You have no way of knowing how you may have helped your friend already. Yes, your friend is getting into trouble, but your prayers might have kept your friend from truly going overboard. You have also told him your concern about some of his actions, and you have shown him a loving attitude. While it might not feel like you've accomplished anything, you probably have. You've let him know you are a true friend. Apart from prayer, that could prove to be the most important thing you do.

I'd like to tell you about my friend Mike. Mike was in a youth group I was leading. In fact, he was a student leader in the group from junior high through the middle of his sophomore year. But then he started living a double life—acting like a Christian at youth group, then partying when he wasn't around his Christian friends. At first he hid his other life pretty well, but eventually some of his friends figured out what was going on.

Several of Mike's friends asked to meet with me so we could talk about the situation. Some of them were mad and disappointed in Mike, but they still loved him and were concerned about him. One night after youth group, I asked Mike if we could get together. He paused, but he said OK.

Over soft drinks at a local restaurant, I said to Mike, "We've known each other for a long time, and I hope you know how much I value your friendship. Several of your Christian friends are worried about you. They are not judging you, but they're simply worried about some of your lifestyle choices." He was very defensive. I just said, "I want you to know that I'm your friend no matter what choices you make, and you can feel free to call me if you ever find yourself in trouble." He left, and I felt like my time with him was a complete failure.

The very next weekend I got a call from Mike at 1 A.M. He asked if I could drive him home from a party. I got up out of bed (reluctantly!) and went to pick him up. I was ready to really let him have it. But Mike was drunk and he wasn't communicating well, so I kept my mouth shut and brought him back to his house. The next morning Mike called and said, "I'm ready to talk." To make a long story short, today Mike is one of the finest youth workers I know.

Not every story has such a great ending. Ultimately, your friend will have to make his own decisions. All you can do is be a faithful friend and good example. And rest assured that God will do his part, too.

32. My Friend's an Atheist

My best friend and I have been friends for five years. I'm a Christian and she's not. I really care about her, and I want her to get to know Jesus. I want her to have the happiness I've found in Christ. Every time I try to talk to her about Jesus, she gets offended and gives me the cold shoulder. She says my beliefs are offensive to her. How can I talk to her about God's truth when she won't listen?

To be honest, the gospel of Jesus Christ is offensive to many non-Christians. After all, Jesus said, "I am the way and the truth and the life. No one comes to the Father except through me" (Jn 14:6). If you aren't following Jesus, that's not very good news.

My guess is you'll need to communicate your faith through actions and commitment instead of words. The apostle John said it best when he said, "Dear children, let us not love with words or tongue but with actions and in truth" (1 Jn 3:18). If I were you, I would maintain a strong friendship with this girl and realize that your witness might take place over years of shared experiences.

I'd like to share a story from my own life. Jerry was a friend of mine from second grade all the way through high school. He was a great guy, and I knew he went to church because he was always busy on Sundays. Although my family didn't go to church and I really didn't understand Jerry's faith, I sensed something was different about him.

After I became a Christian in high school, I asked Jerry about his faith, and he told me that he and his family had prayed for me since second grade. I looked back on my friendship with Jerry and saw several ways he planted the seed of faith in my life. He was a faithful friend. He showed me he cared about me by taking an interest in my life. And he was consistent in his faith, showing me what it was to live as a Christian. I imagine Jerry and his family had hoped I would become a Christian much sooner than I did, but God's timing is different than our timing and God's ways are different than our ways. In God's eyes, I became a Christian at just the right time.

You can be like Jerry. You can be faithful to God and continue to be an excellent witness to your friend. Even though she may not say it, she is watching you and listening to you. She is forming her opinions about Christianity based on what she sees in you and other Christians. Don't be afraid to share your personal faith experiences with her once in a while. After all, she is your friend, and friends talk about what is most important in their lives. Your influence may not end up leading your friend to Christ, but you will have been obedient and shown her what it means to be a Christian.

That doesn't mean you have to be perfect. Too often, Christians think they can only be good witnesses if they act like they never struggle or fail. But nothing is further from the truth. Christians stumble all the time. That's why we so desperately need God in our lives every day. If you make a mistake, let your friend see you deal with your failing, ask for forgiveness and move on with God's help. That honest expression of faith can often say more to a non-Christian than any sermon.

Let me also mention two cautions. As I said, it's natural and perfectly acceptable for you to talk about the things God is doing in your life. But don't try to convince your friend that she needs to accept Christ as her Savior right now. While that's part of the truth she needs to hear someday, it's clear she isn't yet open to the gospel.

My other caution is this: Don't go it alone. Make sure you have solid Christian friends surrounding you to keep you strong in your own life. If you're not already, get involved in your church youth group or a Christian club at your school. Talk to your youth leader about your friend and ask him or her to pray with you periodically. And if your parents are Christians, include them in your witness to your friend.

You may never see the fruit of your efforts to share Christ with your friend. But trust that God is using you right now to help her find the way, the truth and the life.

33. I Want Other Friends, Too

I have a friend who gets very jealous when I spend time with other people. If I'm talking to someone else, she'll join the conversation, then say things to make me look bad. I'm annoyed with her, but I don't know what to do about it. She's had a difficult life, and I don't want to hurt her. How should I deal with her?

Your friend is needy. Like most needy people, she's doing things she knows will get her the attention she craves. The irony is that people who interrupt and put others down in front of friends often lose friendships—the very thing they desperately want. I want to encourage you to continue to be compassionate toward her.

What she needs is a gentle confrontation from you. A true friend is one who will be honest, who will bring up a difficult issue in a caring way. I want to challenge you to actually take the uncomfortable road. Sit down with her to tell her how you feel when she interrupts your conversations. Though this won't be easy, it will help her understand your feelings and, frankly, may save your relationship with her. If you don't talk with her about this ongoing problem, my guess is your friendship with her will deteriorate because of your frustration.

Confrontation is a difficult but necessary part of all growing friendships. For those of us who always want other people to feel good and like us, it's especially difficult. We're afraid that if we do tell our friends the truth, we'll hurt their feelings. They may even reject us. Actually, my experience is that if you are sensitive and caring, neither usually happens. My experience tells me that if I don't share my true feelings with a friend, those feelings will eventually come out in anger, or I'll find myself giving the person the "cold shoulder."

As you consider confronting your friend, keep two principles in mind. The first is to tell the truth in love (see Eph 4:15). By caring enough to share your feelings in a loving way, you'll show how much her friendship really means to you. When you talk to your friend, be careful not to blame her or accuse her of being jealous; instead explain your frustrations, then assure her you want to have her in your life. You might say something like, "I really value your friendship, but it hurts my feelings when you interrupt me or say things about me that make me look bad."

But you need to do more than just say the right things—you need to say them for the right reasons. That's the second principle: Confront because you care. Don't just talk about this issue because you're annoyed with your friend. Talk about it with her because you genuinely want to build a stronger friendship with her.

When I was a church youth worker several years ago, one of my staff members confronted me about how I was "manipulating" people. My first reaction was one of anger at him. Who was he to tell me? In my mind I immediately went over all his faults and problems. But you know, the more I thought about his concerns, the more I realized he was right. He had pointed out a character flaw I definitely needed to work on. Today I am grateful that he told me the truth in love and that he honestly cared enough to confront me with a flaw in my life.

By gently confronting your friend, you are giving her a gift many never receive but desperately need—the gift of an honest friendship. Who knows—maybe she will open up and share the insecurities that cause her to act out her jealous feelings in the first place.

34. My Friend's Dad Is Dying

My friend's father has an incurable brain tumor. My friend has always been a strong Christian, but now she's having all kinds of doubts. She's really angry at God, yelling and swearing at him for ruining her life. How can I help her keep her faith?

Your friend is experiencing something very normal: grief. Grief is our response to pain and tragedy. And each person grieves in a different way. When my mom died I wasn't angry at God, but I had an overwhelming sense of sadness. Others in my family were angry and, like your friend, took that anger out on God.

Just because your friend is angry at God right now doesn't mean she's going to be angry forever. She doesn't need someone to tell her that her feelings are bad, or that God won't love her if she swears at him. She's got enough to deal with already without feeling like she's doing something wrong. Instead, your friend needs to see the love of God through you. Now is the time for you to almost literally be the hands and arms and voice of God. As she deals with the grief of her father's brain tumor, she will need someone like you to just listen to her and be a steady, positive, Christian presence.

It can be very difficult to hear people blame God and shout at him, but I honestly believe he can take it. Look at Psalm 22, where David cries out in anguish to God, wondering why God doesn't rescue him from his pain and despair. If God can handle David's anger, he can handle your friend's anger, too. I also believe God understands your friend's pain. God knows what it feels like to lose a loved one. Remember, he watched his only Son die on the cross.

So be a living example of God's care and tenderness for your friend. Love her, listen to her, pray for her, and hopefully, she'll find comfort in God's love.

35. Mixing Friends

There's a new girl in my school who's fun, funny and sweet. The problem is none of my other friends like her. They insult her and make fun of her. I'm just about her only friend. But I can't hang out with her and my other friends at the same time. How can I be friends with both sides?

The way you describe the new girl, she sounds like a pretty neat person. And your other friends sound a little jealous of her. Whatever you do, be sure you don't stoop to their level of petty insults. True friends rise above the temptation to tease and instead find the good in each person.

Even though your friends hurl insults at your new friend, you can take a stand and make a difference by continuing to be her friend. Eventually, your old friends may tire of their pettiness and follow your lead. Frankly, a loyal friend is hard to find and a lot of people will respect you for your stand.

I believe every person is created by God and should be treated with respect. I don't have to hang around with everyone, but when I look at each person who comes into my life as a child of God, it's easier to be kind to them. At this point your friends have the problem, not you. I want to challenge you to set an example and lead them toward kindness.

36. I Need Someone to Listen

My friends always talk to me about their problems. I'm glad they trust me and know they can lean on me, but I'm getting really irritated with them. They never ask me how I am, or how I'm doing. I'm pretty independent and secure, so I guess they think I can handle my own problems. But I feel like I give and give, and never get anything back from them. How can I get my friends to see that I sometimes need them, too?

Tell them. It's wonderful you are a person others can talk to. But sometimes you just need to lay the cards on the table and share *your* burdens with your friends. They need to know you need them, too.

Some people just don't think about other people's problems; they're too busy with their own pain. That doesn't mean they don't care about others; it just doesn't always occur to them to ask about their friends' lives. You seem to have the intuition to ask about your friends' problems. That's why people expect you to be the listener and not the person in need of help. But as you're discovering, that can be frustrating.

I've been in your shoes. Lots of people come to me to talk about their problems. But, like everyone else, I have struggles of my own to talk about. For me, the best place to do this is in a support group at my church. This small group gets together once a week to spend time sharing and praying for each other. Because I'm able to talk openly about myself in the group, I feel I'm better prepared to counsel my friends.

If you continue to experience the frustration you feel now, it will become more and more difficult for you to be the caring friend you want to be. By leaning on others for support when you need it, you'll be an even better source of help to your friends. So it's important for you to meet regularly with a small group of friends who can bring you support and encouragement. If you don't know where to find such a group, ask your youth pastor for help. Ask if you can team up with others who can offer you not only a shoulder to lean on, but a chance to air your frustrations and receive wise counsel and advice.

You may also want to take a look at the people you hang around with. If all your friends are needy, I suggest you actively pursue a few friendships where there is some mutual give-and-take in the relationship. Several years ago I was feeling really drained and friendless. Then I looked at the people I was spending time with. Almost all of them were people who demanded a lot of attention from me. For some reason I was surrounded by needy people. I realized I needed a few friends who would fill me up, rather than drain me. Sure, these people have their share of problems, but they're also friends who show an interest in my life.

Good, caring friends are hard to find. Your friends are fortunate to have you in their lives. I wish you the best as you find a few more friends who can offer you the same support you've given to others.

37. Call Me When You've Got It Together

My former best friend has gotten into all kinds of serious trouble in the last year or so. She's started doing hard drugs like cocaine, and she's become sexually promiscuous. She got pregnant by one of her many partners and had an abortion. I told her these things were too much for me to handle all at once. I just couldn't watch her slowly killing herself, not to mention ending her baby's life. I told her to call me when she wanted to get her life together. We've talked once since then, and she promised to change—but she hasn't. Was I wrong not to support her? How long should you stand by a friend who just keeps getting deeper and deeper into trouble?

This friend of yours is going through some very serious struggles. She needs people like you to be there as she considers her life choices and hopefully, one day, her ultimate decision to follow God's plan for her life. As hard as it is for you to watch her make bad decisions, it's important for her sake, and for yours, that you be a friend she can count on.

It is possible to be in a relationship with someone and still let them know you disapprove of their lifestyle. Sometimes you don't even have to use words. Just by refusing to take part in those activities that clash with your values, and by modeling a more Christlike way of life, you can make a difference.

You asked me the question, "How long should you stand by a friend who just keeps getting deeper and deeper into trouble?" Let me answer it by asking you two questions. If you were that girl, how long would you hope a Christian friend would stand by you? How long would Jesus stand by her? I think you have the answer in your heart.

I'm sure the relationship is complicated and you could tell me some stories of how you have tried to reach your friend. Let me just encourage you not to give up on her. God won't give up, and he may just use you to get his message of love and forgiveness across to her.

38. Don't Go There!

Last year, I was in the middle of every piece of gossip and every fight my friends had. People kept telling me what everyone said and asking me for help. It all really dragged me down. When school starts again, how can I keep supporting my friends and still get them to handle their own problems?

I have two teenage daughters who struggle with the same issue. When one of them asked my advice, I gave her my three-word formula: "Don't go there!" It's the same thing I tell myself when I get into a similar situation. I look for an escape route and get out. Sometimes the "escape" is as easy as changing the subject. At other times, you literally have to leave the situation.

I also gave my daughter two Scriptures that have really helped me. Jesus' advice was, "Watch and pray so that you will not fall into temptation. The spirit is willing, but the body is weak" (Mt 26:41). Paul reminds us, "No temptation has seized you except what is common to man. And God is faithful; he will not let you be tempted beyond what you can bear. But when you are tempted, he will also provide a way out so that you can stand up under it" (1 Cor 10:13). That last verse holds a great promise for you and me. Claim it when you are in the middle of one of those gossip or fight sessions.

Still, to this day, I don't always follow my own advice. But it helps me when I read the note my daughter has pinned to the bulletin board in her room. It reads, in her handwriting, "Don't Go There!"

THREE

Self-Image

39. How Can I Lose Weight?

I am fifteen years old. I'm 5'5" tall and I weigh 250 lbs. My doctor says I'm not healthy, but no matter how hard I try I can't lose weight. What can I do? I'm tired of being made fun of!

When it comes to weight loss and eating disorders, there are no easy answers. But here are a few things I encourage you to try.

Get a complete physical. When you want to lose weight, make sure you do it under the care of a physician. There is no such thing as a quick fix or diet fad that will help you instantly lose weight. If the doctor doesn't find anything physically wrong with you (like a thyroid condition) that's causing weight gain, then with his or her help move to the next step.

Choose a healthy weight loss plan. Find a plan that works for you. The best plans will help you learn a new way of eating and exercising and will also provide you with accountability. I have a friend who enrolled in the Weight Watchers program, which challenged him to exercise daily and eat right. He asked me to be his accountability partner. My job was to cheer him on with his victories and help him stay focused after a defeat. Sure, he had some setbacks, but a year later he had lost weight and now feels better than ever. Find an accountability partner to help you through what, at fifteen, could be one of the most challenging yet victorious times of your life. This person needs to be loving and caring yet brutally honest.

Seek counsel. The Bible says, "For lack of guidance a nation falls, but many advisers make victory sure" (Prv 11:14). In addition to choosing the right weight loss plan, get counseling to help you understand how you reached this point. A counselor can help you decide if you have a common problem called "compulsive eating disorder," where people try to cope with their problems by eating a lot. And these people really can't overcome their eating disorder until they figure out the causes behind it. A trained counselor can often help them get to the root of their problem. As a result, this can lead to a more effective way of losing weight.

Seek God's help. God created your body and he can give you the strength to help you overcome your circumstances. My friend who's done so well this past year recently stood up at church and said, "This has been the best year of my life. I want to acknowledge God's presence. I couldn't have done it on my own."

You also won't be able to do it alone. But God doesn't expect you to. Through Christ, he will give you the strength you need (see Phil 4:13).

40. I Overeat

I've had this problem for a long time: I overeat. It makes me feel good for a while, but then I start feeling disgusting and depressed. Then I hate myself and the cycle starts again. I constantly ask God for help and forgiveness, but I feel so hopeless and out of control. I'm attractive and have a lot going for me, but I can't seem to conquer this problem. How can I give God control over my eating habits?

It sounds to me like you've got an eating disorder. I have a medical dictionary that defines eating disorders as "disturbances in eating behavior that result in injury to a person's physical or psychological health." That seems to be what's happening to you.

The particular eating disorder you've described is what experts call "compulsive overeating." Compulsive overeaters use food the same way some people use alcohol or other drugs to deal with stress, or to dull depression, anger or other difficult emotions. Most compulsive overeaters consume food for emotional reasons rather than hunger, and feel out of control around food. While other eating disorders such as anorexia nervosa and bulimia may be more well-known, compulsive overeating is by far the most common eating disorder.

Here are some symptoms of a compulsive overeater:
- alternating between compulsive overeating and chronic dieting
- bingeing (overeating) without purging (vomiting)
- eating for emotional reasons instead of hunger
- guilt feelings
- self-hatred

If you think you have some of these symptoms, and it sounds as though you do, I suggest you have a very open discussion about this problem with either your doctor, a school counselor or a professional Christian counselor. They can help determine the severity of your problem and help you take steps toward recovery.

While you're receiving the needed help from a counselor, you also need to seek God's guidance. God doesn't expect you to conquer this difficult problem by yourself. He wants to help you and promises he'll be there to guide you. Check out Psalm 119, Jeremiah 29:11 and Matthew 28:20 for God's promises to be with you.

You can also take some other practical steps to start the recovery process. The best advice I can give you is to take it one day, one hour at a time. You don't need to promise to never overeat again; just promise to make it through the next hour. When you succeed, great. If you experience a setback, it's only for that hour. Give yourself some grace and start again.

You may also want to find a trusted friend who can be your accountability partner. When you feel tempted to overeat, call this friend. When you blow it, call them. If you had a good day, call them. Your accountability partner can help keep you on track and cheer you on when you resist temptation.

With God's help, a good counselor and an accountability partner you trust, you'll be on your way to gaining control over your eating and living a healthy life.

41. Food Controls Me

It seems like I've obsessed over food for as long as I can remember. My dissatisfaction with the way I look has caused me to try all kinds of things, like diet pills and even suicide. A year ago, I decided the best way to stay thin was to throw up after meals. I felt I could control my life. But now I wake up every morning worried about what I will eat and where the nearest bathroom is. I want Christ to be the center of my life, not food. Please help me!

At one time or another most all of us use food to comfort us when we are down. But it sounds like your obsessive-compulsive eating habits are at a dangerous level of physical, mental and spiritual health.

I urge you to get help now. Talk with a counselor who understands eating disorders and ask them for the help you truly need to work on this issue. I want to give you some information on eating disorders in the next few paragraphs, but again, I strongly recommend that you share your struggle with a counselor *right away.*

The term "eating disorder" is used by medical or mental-health professionals to describe a person's obsession with food and weight, or inappropriate eating behavior. Two common types of eating disorders are anorexia and bulimia. From the sound of your letter, you may have bulimia and possibly anorexia as well. Let me define the terms. Anorexia is an emotional disorder involving self-starvation that produces an extremely thin body. Bulimia is a pattern of gorging and purging the food, usually through self-induced vomiting. Let me be very serious with you: Anorexia and bulimia can be fatal.

Common side effects include damage to reproductive organs, abnormal heart and metabolic rates, and heart and kidney failure. In other words, an eating disorder can be very dangerous and needs immediate attention.

You mentioned that you want Christ to be the center of your life—not food. A small, close-knit support group can help you keep your commitment to Christ strong and help you with your eating temptations as well. I love the promise of God that says, "For where two or three come together in my name, there am I with them" (Mt 18:20). Jesus Christ loves you and cares about your food issue even more than you do. Seek him first and allow him to help you replace your cravings for food and your struggle with body image with a healthy commitment to Christ.

The following are organizations you can contact to get the help you need:

Overcomers Outreach
(714) 491-3000
www.overcomersoutreach.org

Rapha
1-800-383-HOPE
www.rapha.org

National Association of Anorexia Nervosa
and Associated Disorders
(847) 831-3438
www.anad.org

42. Remaining Guilt

I've been struggling with an eating disorder for a while. I've been in counseling for a few months and am slowly getting better. But I still feel a lot of guilt because of how I've hurt my body, the temple of God. I feel like I've let God down because it's so hard for me to love myself as I am, as the person he made me. What can I do to get rid of this guilt?

As you probably already know from counseling, people who struggle with eating disorders are often very much alike. They are perfectionists, who can never measure up to their very high expectations of themselves. These same people also sometimes have trouble accepting the unconditional love of God. It sounds like you might be that type of person. That's why I can't stress enough that God loves you not for what you do, but for who you are—his child. God's love and acceptance of you knows no limits or boundaries. He sent his Son, Jesus Christ, to die for you so you could receive his grace.

Grace and mercy are sometimes difficult to accept. Grace means "unmerited favor." But the world works in the opposite way: You get what you deserve—no more, no less. Thankfully, God's ways are not our ways. Even though we have all made mistakes, Jesus Christ reaches out his nail-pierced hands to us and says, "I love you." He offers us unmerited favor. Your image of God is missing an important piece: He is the heavenly Father who wants to provide grace to the children he loves. And that includes you.

On the practical side, I want to offer three short suggestions:

1. Stay close to people who show and offer you grace. They could be people in your youth group or just one or two special friends. Either way, they should be people who show you what it means to practice love and forgiveness.
2. Keep up the counseling. Getting over an eating disorder isn't easy. Neither is learning to walk in God's grace. If your counselor is a Christian, talk to him or her about your struggles with your faith. If your counselor isn't a Christian, talk with your pastor or youth pastor about God's grace. As you learn more about God's love for you, I think you'll also learn to love yourself.
3. Memorize a few Bible verses on God's grace and love. Here are my top four:

- *"For God so loved the world that he gave his one and only Son, that whoever believes in him shall not perish but have eternal life"* (Jn 3:16).
- *"But God demonstrates his own love for us in this: While we were still sinners, Christ died for us"* (Rom 5:8).
- *"Who shall separate us from the love of Christ? Shall trouble or hardship or persecution or famine or nakedness or danger or sword? ... No, in all these things we are more than conquerors through him who loved us"* (Rom 8:35, 37).
- *"If we confess our sins, he is faithful and just and will forgive us our sins and purify us from all unrighteousness"* (1 Jn 1:9).

As you do these things and read these verses, I think you'll begin to feel more deserving of God's love and grace.

43. I'm Just Too Skinny

I'm 5'6" and weigh only ninety pounds. I know there are overweight people who think I'm lucky, but the truth is people make fun of me all the time. They say I'm bulimic and anorexic. I eat plenty and I'm very healthy, but I don't seem to gain weight. My family tells me to just laugh it off, but the harsh words people say really hurt. How can I gain more self-confidence so the things people say won't hurt me so much?

You are thin for your height. I checked in with a doctor I know and he agreed it would be wise for you to get a very thorough physical examination. You might want to go to a specialist called an endocrinologist—a doctor who specializes in hormones. The doctor can make certain there are no physical problems keeping you from gaining weight.

Also, keep in mind that during your teenage years, physical development happens fast. Once you're sure there are no health concerns, the best you can do is wait for your body to grow and change. You may experience a major growth spurt, complete with weight gain, any day. It could happen tomorrow, it could happen years from now. You may even be thin because of your genetic makeup. Is the rest of your family on the thin side? If so, there's very little you can do to change the shape of your body.

I would also encourage you to keep eating a healthy diet. It might be tempting to load up on junk food in the hope you'll put on weight. But in the long run, you'll do your body more harm than good.

Once you've seen a doctor and been given a clean bill of

health, I think you should take your family's advice. It may be difficult to laugh off the harsh words, but there's very little you can do to change the things other people say. All you can change is your reaction to them.

If you're doing everything you can to be healthy, it's time to accept the fact that for now, you're thin. Here's a scripture that has helped me along the way with things I don't necessarily love about my body. These words don't make our physical issues go away, but they can remind us of who made us and that we are all unique in God's eyes:

> For you created my inmost being; you knit me together in my mother's womb. I praise you because I am fearfully and wonderfully made; your works are wonderful, I know that full well. My frame was not hidden from you when I was made in the secret place. When I was woven together in the depths of the earth, your eyes saw my unformed body. All the days ordained for me were written in your book before one of them came to be.
>
> PSALM 139:13-16

44. Why Am I Depressed?

I'm depressed. I feel like nobody loves me, and I always put myself down. I'm not a really bad person or anything, so I'm not sure why this is happening. What's wrong with me?

Nothing, maybe. But it sounds like you've made the mistake of viewing depression as the direct result of repeated faults or individual sins. Depression is a complex condition that has physical, emotional, psychological and spiritual aspects. It's not a punishment for wrongdoing, nor is it a sign of weakness or a character flaw.

Depression occurs more frequently among teenagers than most people realize, and it ranges from negative feelings to thinking seriously about suicide. In fact, depression is a very common medical condition in all age groups. One-fourth of all women and 12 percent of men in the United States will go through it. There's no clear answer why some people get depressed and others don't.

The first question here is not why you're depressed, but if you're depressed—in the clinical/medical sense, that is. Generally speaking, depression can include:

- feelings of sadness
- loss of interest in once-enjoyed activities
- changes in appetite or weight
- changes in sleeping patterns
- restlessness
- decreased activity that is noticeable to others
- fatigue or loss of energy
- difficulty concentrating or making decisions
- feelings of worthlessness or inappropriate guilt
- recurrent thoughts of death or suicide

If you've experienced some of these symptoms for two weeks or more, there's a good chance you are depressed. Assuming this does describe you, talk with a professional counselor or your doctor. Don't try to climb out of depression alone.

Along with seeking professional help, you should read the Bible—the Psalms are especially helpful. Exercise and time spent with fun-loving friends are a must as well.

God meets us even in our darkest moments. Here are two of God's incredible promises to encourage you:

> The Lord is my shepherd, I shall not be in want. He makes me lie down in green pastures, he leads me beside quiet waters, he restores my soul.
>
> PSALM 23:1-3

> I will never leave you or forsake you.
>
> HEBREWS 13:5, NKJV

45. I Feel So Alone

Every day, it seems like I'm learning to love God more and more. But I still feel very lonely. I'm not very close to my family. I feel like they barely know me, and I find them hard to talk to. I try to talk with my friends, but I feel like they don't really listen to me. Even though I try to find refuge in God, I still feel so alone. I don't know what to do.

Loneliness is a difficult thing. And it's something felt by a great number of people. In a time when people move often, spend less time with their families and struggle to find a place to really "belong," loneliness is bound to creep in. Even with your growing faith and the knowledge that God is in your life, you still feel the need for deepened relationships with family and friends.

Your letter reminds me of a girl in my youth group named Christie. She seemed to have everything going for her. She was smart, attractive and involved in her school and church activities. One day, after a Bible study on loneliness, she came up to me and told me she didn't feel like she had anyone she could talk to. I was completely surprised. She said, "All my friendships are superficial. Most nights I sit home by myself."

As we talked, Christie made three really smart decisions. First, she decided to join a small group of girls at the church who got together to pray and talk once a week. She didn't wait for them to invite her; she just asked if she could join them, and they were happy to have her. Second, she decided to find times to talk with her parents and tell them about the things going on in her life. They had assumed she was content and enjoying her life; she wanted them to know that wasn't always true. And third, she began to accept the fact that loneliness is a part of many of our lives, but that we can use those times to grow closer to God.

Christie's small prayer group became a major part of her life. Not only did the group pray together, but they found themselves talking on the phone and doing social things throughout the week as well. Eventually, Christie even felt comfortable talking with her friends about times of intense loneliness.

Christie mentioned that she wished she had a better relationship with her parents. One of the girls suggested that Christie schedule "date nights" with her parents. Christie began to look for ways to initiate activities with her parents together and separately. She found that when she and her dad went to get a hamburger at his favorite burger joint, he would share with her more personally about his life and listen more closely when she talked about her life. She and her mom began to walk together in the mornings, and these walks became Christie's special times to connect with her mom.

After that first conversation, Christie and I periodically talked about her loneliness. We talked about how many people she knew tried to cover up their empty feelings of loneliness with drugs and alcohol or sexual promiscuity. I encouraged Christie to continue seeking God's best for her life. I also recommended she take a close look at the Book of Psalms. David, who wrote many of the psalms, was sorting through all kinds of emotions, including loneliness, as he wrote. Christie found several pPsalms that gave her comfort when she was feeling lonely. I want to encourage you to do the same. They won't always make your feelings of loneliness disappear, but many of the psalms will remind you of God's presence in your life.

I hope you'll try some of Christie's ideas and continue to seek God's refuge. He'll not only comfort you when you're feeling alone, but he'll also lead you to deepened relationships with others.

46. I Need Higher Self-Esteem

I've been struggling a lot with my self-esteem, which is low, and I find myself depending on what people think of me. I don't want to be a really proud person, but I also need better self-esteem. How can I find it?

Here's a really simple answer for a great question: You'll find your proper self-image in a solid understanding of the love of God. Am I saying it's easy to overcome an inferiority complex? Can you learn to feel good about yourself in ten simple lessons? The answer is an emphatic NO. God never promised us a life free from struggles.

But I have some great news for you. You *can* establish your own identity and learn to really like yourself. And better yet, building a healthy self-image is not all your responsibility.

The God who created this world cares deeply about who you are and who you are becoming. This is the way I figure it: To build a healthy self-image in you, God must do his part and you must do yours. God's already done his part. He created you, loves you, forgives you, accepts you and values you. He's given you unique gifts and talents.

Let's expand on these things God has done for you. God created you, so he knows you fully and loves you. Through Jesus Christ, he forgives you and accepts you as his child. He values your relationship with him enough to sacrifice his only Son for you, so you can have an abundant life on earth and an eternal relationship with God. He's gifted you with abilities that will benefit his kingdom and make you a healthy, joyful person. I've heard it said this way: "God don't sponsor no flops." So you see, helping you learn to like yourself is at the very core of what God wants to do in you and through you.

That's God's part in this picture. Your part is simply to respond to what God has already done for you. You need to accept this incredible love of God in your life and serve his kingdom. All your problems won't go away, but the core of your self-image will be much stronger.

47. I Love Others, Just Not Myself

As a Christian, I realize we're supposed to love others, and I do. My problem is loving myself. I look at myself in the mirror and hate what I see. I know this isn't what God wants, and that thinking I'm ugly and fat goes against what it says in the Bible about being fearfully and wonderfully made. But I just can't help it. I've prayed about this so much, but I still cannot find any love for myself. Please help.

You're not alone. Most of us struggle with a poor self-image at times. When I'm feeling less than positive about myself, there's a prayer by Reinhold Neiburh I like to read. It simply states: "God grant me the serenity to accept the things I cannot change; courage to change the things I can; and wisdom to know the difference." That's great advice for anyone struggling with self-esteem.

You might be able to change some things you don't like about yourself. Ask God to give you the strength and help to change those things. But there might also be things you can't change. Ask God to help you accept those things. This prayer can help you learn to love yourself just the way God created you.

To be honest, from reading your letter, you probably know in your mind all the stuff I just wrote. For lots of people, the teenage years are the most difficult time to have a positive self-image. It's just not easy growing up in our media-driven culture. There are so many messages that tell you to look and act a certain way, and if you don't measure up (and honestly, no one does), it's easy to feel like a loser.

But no matter what our culture says, God's love remains the

same. He loves you just the way you are. He is proud of his creation. You are unique. According to Scripture, you are God's workmanship (see Eph 2:10). God's love for you is unconditional, unchanging and unending.

My best advice is to begin moving your "head knowledge" of God's love and acceptance down a few inches, making it "heart knowledge." Find friends who will reinforce your faith and values and who will be a support to you. Fill your heart with the knowledge of God's love and find friends who lift you up rather than pull you down. When you do, you'll begin to see that you are a special and unique person created by God for life abundant and eternal.

48. Playing the Comparison Game

I constantly compare myself to other people. God has gifted me in many areas, but it seems like I always have to be "the best" to feel good about myself. I am rarely satisfied. I know God wants me to be content with myself, and I try to be happy with who I am, but it's hard. How can I stop being so competitive?

Believe me, you aren't the only one with this problem. So many people are caught up in the comparison game. But that's a game we always lose. It isn't difficult to find someone who's smarter or more attractive or a better athlete than we are. Many of us feel the pressure to be "the best." And that pressure, as you know, is tough to take.

Where does this competitive, perfectionist, never-quite-satisfied attitude come from? I think a lot of it is connected to a bad self-image. So many of us have a poor view of ourselves. We're convinced we're no good, that we have nothing to offer. So we knock ourselves out trying to be the best at something, just so we can feel a little better about ourselves.

And striving for perfection isn't a new thing. The Bible is full of people trying to please God and society with their actions. Remember the parable of the Pharisee and the tax collector in Luke 18? As the Pharisee prays, he tells God about his "righteous" acts, like tithing and fasting. He's trying to prove to God (and anyone else who might be listening) that he's perfect. But the parable points out that God is more concerned with what's in our hearts than with our attempts to be perfect. God loves each of us for who we are, not what we do.

You are a child of God with all the rights and privileges of any other child of God. And you know he has gifted you with specific talents and spiritual gifts. And it would be wonderful if you could accept yourself just as God made you and not compare yourself with anything or anyone else. But head knowledge is one thing; living out that knowledge is another.

To help the message of God's love sink in, I'd like you to try a few things. First, think about what the Bible says about you. It says you are created in the image of God himself (see Gn 1:26). It says you are "fearfully and wonderfully made" (Ps 139:14). And it says God's love for you is sacrificial and unconditional. Romans 5:8 says, "God demonstrates his own love for us in this: While we were still sinners, Christ died for us." God loves you just the way you are.

With those passages in mind, think about these questions:

1. *What are your spiritual gifts?* Look at Romans 12:6-8 to find out how God wants us to use our gifts. Then look for opportunities to use yours.

2. *What talents has God given you?* Thank God for blessing you with these abilities and use them for him.

3. *How would you feel if you gave someone a gift and they responded by saying, "It's OK, but it's not as nice as the one you gave my brother"?* That's essentially what we're saying to God when we compare ourselves with others. Whenever you find yourself playing the comparison game, stop and thank God for what you have, instead of dwelling on what you haven't.

4. *Who are three positive, enthusiastic people you can talk to about this issue?* Find those people and ask them to help you. If you can't think of anyone, you may want to consider talking to a Christian counselor. I've found that sitting with someone who really knows how to listen and offer wisdom is great way to receive insight on my self-image.

As you answer these questions, I think you'll begin to see that you are indeed "wonderfully made."

49. My Complexion Is Killing My Self-Image

I hate the way I look. I have really bad acne. I've been going to the dermatologist, and that's helping some, but I still hate the way I look. I've prayed that God would heal me, but he hasn't answered my prayer. I sometimes lose faith in God because of the way I look and feel. I've even thought about suicide. I want to live, but not like this. What can I do?

I wish I could put you in touch with our family friend, who I'll call Janet. She is an adult now, but during high school and college her situation was similar to yours. It wasn't easy for Janet. Her acne deeply affected her self-image. She didn't date or even make friends easily. Like you, she questioned God, prayed for healing, argued, bargained and cried. But ultimately, she was able to make peace with her appearance, and with God.

Janet helped me with this answer. Our advice to you is based on her experience, and we hope you'll take it to heart.

The first thing we want to say is this: Please don't attempt suicide. Suicide is a permanent solution to a temporary problem. If you ever start to make a plan for killing yourself or actually try to hurt yourself, please seek help from a qualified Christian counselor. If you feel suicidal urges and don't know where to turn, get to the emergency room of your local hospital. They'll be able to help you through the immediate crisis.

Janet and I also recommend these ideas to help you feel better about yourself:

Remember, you aren't that different from most other people. Take a good look at your classmates. Are any of them perfect physical specimens? No. They may not struggle with acne, but I'm sure most of them are self-conscious about some aspect of their appearance. I don't want to downplay your feelings, but you can find some comfort in knowing you're not alone in wishing you could change the way you look.

Keep working with your dermatologist. A dermatologist I know says the recent breakthroughs are incredibly positive and effective.

Focus on what's positive about you. You are so much more than just a face; you are a precious child of God. You have gifts and talents that can enrich the lives of other people. What do you like to do? What are you good at? What are some of the good things going on in your life? Don't get so worried about your burdens that you forget to count your many blessings.

Think about the future. You won't be in high school forever. Sure, there will always be people who'll judge you based on the way you look. But as you get older, you'll meet more and more people who will appreciate you for who you are and not for what you look like.

Lean on God. When you're feeling bad about yourself, tell God. Ask him to comfort you and give you strength to deal with your problem. God may not heal your acne, but he will heal your emotional pain, if you let him.

Read 1 Samuel 16:1-13. God says to Samuel, 'Do not consider his appearance or his height, for I have rejected him. The Lord does not look at the things man looks at. Man looks at the outward appearance, but the Lord looks at the heart" (1 Sm 16:7). God is much more concerned about a person's inner qualities than that person's appearance. When I start feeling bad about the way I look (see, you really aren't alone), I go to that verse and try to get perspective.

I hope you can begin to see that God cares for you and wants you to grow closer to him in the midst of your struggles.

50. My Friend Doesn't Like Herself

My best friend has really low self-esteem. I've tried to help her, but nothing seems to work. She thinks my other friends and I are lying to her whenever we compliment her. What can I do?

There's not much you can do or say to change someone's mind about their self-image. But you can make a difference by being a caring and supportive friend. When your friend knows you are there for her, regardless of how she feels about herself, her personal outlook can begin to change.

For example, consider Jennifer. She once said: "I hate myself. I'm ugly, I'm stupid and I can't even imagine that God would love a person like me."

Enter Robin.

Robin stuck by her and by being a good friend showed her the love of God. As Jennifer grew and matured, her self-image began to change.

Today Jennifer is one of the key female youth speakers in America. She has often said, "I wouldn't be the person I am today if it weren't for Robin."

God loves us unconditionally, not for what we do but for who we are. God promises that he will never leave us nor forsake us (see Heb 13:5). When we finally grasp that concept, we can be free to like who we are because we know and believe God's promises. Share this verse with your friend, plus a few others like Genesis 1:27, 31; Psalm 139:13-16 and Ephesians 2:10. The Bible is an excellent resource. Use it to help your friend.

51. I Dream Up Ways to Die

I think I might be depressed. I often daydream about jumping off of cliffs and bridges. Sometimes when I feel sad, I turn off all my lights and listen to hard rock music with explicit lyrics. I feel like I can't talk to anyone about my problems because everyone around me has problems of their own. Am I depressed or am I just looking for attention?

I think you're depressed. All of us feel intense sadness at times, but it sounds like there's something more going on with you.

You mention thoughts of jumping off cliffs and bridges. Those kinds of thoughts aren't all that unusual. Many teenagers have daydreams and thoughts of suicide. But if you've actually considered acting on your daydreams, if you've planned a time, a place or a method for killing yourself, I beg you to get help NOW. Talk to a Christian counselor or a counselor at your school.

Even if you're not suicidal, it's important for you to deal with your depression. You might be surprised to know that many people experience feelings of depression at some point in their lives. One friend of mine who counsels teenagers told me depression is the most common problem among the students he works with.

The first thing you need to do is talk with your family doctor. Depression is often brought on by hormones. Your doctor might be able to help you come up with a plan to help you feel better. And an exam will rule out any serious physical reasons for your feelings.

I'd also suggest you stay away from the kind of music you've been listening to. All music affects our moods. It can cheer us up or mellow us out. But the music you're listening to is playing in to your emotions. To be honest, when I'm sad or depressed, my first impulse is to listen to hard-driving, secular rock music that seems like it can help me release some of my own anger and sadness.

But over the years, I've learned that it's exactly the type of music I *shouldn't* listen to when I'm down. It only feeds into my hopelessness. It certainly doesn't offer me any positive alternative to what I'm feeling. Now, I choose to listen to Christian music instead. It builds me up instead of tearing me down. It offers me hope and comfort instead of more anger and despair.

There's all kinds of Christian music out there. You can find Christian bands that offer the sound you like without the explicit lyrics you mentioned. Look for songs that inspire you, that help you focus on the ways God can work in your life. A local Christian music store can be a great place to find the music you want with the message you need.

You don't say anything about your relationship with God. If you're a Christian, I hope you'll bring this problem to your youth pastor, your pastor or a qualified Christian counselor. If you're not a Christian, I still encourage you to talk with a Christian counselor. Depression often arises from an empty spiritual life. But God cares deeply about you, and that includes your feelings. Ask the person you talk with to help you find Scripture references and other devotional materials that can help you feel hopeful about your life. I'd start with Jeremiah 29:11, where God promises he's always in control and wants only the best for you.

You may also want to dig into the Book of Psalms. This is the "praise book" of the Hebrew people. And if you think it's impossible for a follower of God to be depressed, the Psalms will change your mind. David used these songs and poems to pour out his deepest emotions before God. They can help you do the same.

I'd like to leave you with Psalm 46. It's one that helps me out when I'm feeling depressed:

God is our refuge and strength, an ever-present help in trouble. Therefore we will not fear, though the earth give way and the mountains fall into the heart of the sea, though its waters roar and foam and the mountains quake with their surging. There is a river whose streams make glad the city of God, the holy place where the Most High dwells. God is within her, she will not fall; God will help her at break of day. Nations are in uproar, kingdoms fall; he lifts his voice, the earth melts. The Lord Almighty is with us; the God of Jacob is our fortress. Come and see the works of the Lord, the desolations he has brought on the earth. He makes wars cease to the ends of the earth; he breaks the bow and shatters the spear, he burns the shields with fire. "Be still, and know that I am God; I will be exalted among the nations, I will be exalted in the earth." The Lord Almighty is with us; the God of Jacob is our fortress.

52. I Feel Worthless

I was sexually abused as a child and also struggled with anorexia for several years. While I've gotten help for both of these problems, I still have a hard time accepting myself. I know Jesus loves me, and I love him, but I can't stand myself. I feel like I'm trash. How can I learn to like myself?

Life hasn't been easy for you. But in the midst of all you've been through, you seem to have made very wise decisions. It's never easy to ask for help, but by doing so, you've taken a tremendous step toward healing. I hope you'll continue to seek help as you go through the healing process.

As you've recognized, the trauma you've been through has had a lasting effect on your self-esteem. While I can't offer any easy answers, I can point you to some words of hope from the Bible. In the Sermon on the Mount in the book of Matthew, Jesus tells his listeners not to worry about life because God takes care of his creations. Jesus describes how God literally cares for each and every bird on earth. Then Jesus says, "Are you not much more valuable than they?" (Mt 6:26). Jesus makes it clear that God has tremendous love for his people.

To make God's love for you feel more real, picture Jesus looking at you. Imagine him speaking to you with intense love and gentleness and maybe even a tear in his eye as he says, "You are so valuable to me. I love you and I created you to know me and to know my love for you." Perhaps he would even reach out with his nail-pierced hands and hold you in his arms. One thing's for sure: When Jesus looks at you, he doesn't see "trash." He sees a person he loves so deeply, he gave up his life for you.

I strongly believe God wants you to know he created you in his image. That means he created you with love and care. And that makes you someone special. The awful things you experienced have affected the way you see yourself, but *nothing* can affect the way God sees you. Romans 8:35-39 says, "Who shall separate us from the love of Christ? Shall troubles or hardship or persecution or famine or nakedness or danger or sword? ... For I am convinced that neither death nor life ... nor anything else in all creation, will be able to separate us from the love of God that is in Christ Jesus our Lord."

You also need to remember that the sexual abuse you suffered was not your fault. You were a victim of an evil act. It's true you can't change circumstances, but there is help and there is hope. You are incredibly courageous to take steps to recover from your abuse.

Your eating disorder was most likely a result of your damaged self-esteem. And as you've recovered from that illness, I hope you've learned that there's no reason to feel guilty about it. You're getting help, and you're trying to take better care of yourself. In breaking out of a dangerous pattern of starvation, you're showing a great deal of strength and determination. God can see your efforts to heal and he will be there for you as you continue that process.

Developing a positive self-image is a lifelong process. You won't wake up one morning and say, "I think I've got it all together now." Your past will always be a part of your life. But God is a more powerful part of your life, and he can heal even the deepest pain.

53. I Hate the Way I Look

I've spent many years hating myself because of my looks. People call me "fat" and "ugly." I've tried new hairstyles, makeup and new clothes, but nothing seems to help. I hate feeling sorry for myself, but I can't help it. It really hurts when people call me names. I'm a caring, loving person, and I know God loves me, but I still feel so depressed about my looks. How can I feel better about myself?

As I read your letter, I wished so badly that we could meet face-to-face and I could just give you a friendly hug. You sound like a fine person—a person who deserves to be reminded she's worth caring about.

I want to tell you a story about a woman I know who once felt much like you do. I hope her story will help you stay focused on the kind of beauty that's truly important.

Sydney was one of those people who had a great personality, but I'll be honest, many people felt she wasn't very attractive. I know Sydney tried to lose weight and I know she was hurt that she didn't get asked on dates. She had a hard time convincing herself that she was a good and lovable person.

But despite her struggles to feel good about herself, Sydney made some very good decisions along the way. She stayed close to God. She worked hard to develop good friendships with guys. She joined a prayer group at church, and she was always one of the first to volunteer to serve when there was a need.

She may not have been the most attractive girl on the outside, but as she grew in her faith and learned more about giving to others, she became radiant on the inside. This doesn't mean she didn't struggle with her self-image, but she kept working on it.

I remember two Scripture passages that were important to Sydney. The first was part of a conversation the Lord had with the prophet Samuel about a good-looking person who lacked inner beauty:

> But the Lord said to Samuel, "Do not consider his appearance or his height, for I have rejected him. The Lord does not look at the things man looks at. Man looks at the outward appearance, but the Lord looks at the heart."
>
> 1 SAMUEL 16:7

The other passage, Psalm 139:13-16, was a reminder to Sydney of who created her:

> For you created my inmost being; you knit me together in my mother's womb. I praise you because I am fearfully and wonderfully made; your works are wonderful, I know that full well. My frame was not hidden from you when I was made in the secret place. When I was woven together in the depths of the earth, your eyes saw my unformed body.

Today, Sydney is happily married with two beautiful children. Sydney teaches Sunday school for the youth group at her church, and the students absolutely love her. Whenever she tells her students about her difficult high school days, they can hardly believe it. She is one of their heroes. And you know what? Although she will never be considered physically beautiful, her inner beauty overflows, making her a very attractive woman on the inside and the outside.

I hope you will follow Sydney's example. Stay faithful to God. Surround yourself with positive Christian friends. When you're hurting, be sure and share your pain with these friends. And find ways to reach out and serve others. If you concentrate on being beautiful to God, your inner beauty will touch everyone you meet.

FOUR

Teen Issues

54. I Am Fed Up With Gossip

I'm really frustrated with all the gossiping I hear at school. I don't want to participate in these conversations, but I don't know if I should speak up. What would you do?

Gossip is like a wildfire. It gets out of control and spreads quickly. The Bible places gossip along the same line as greed, sexual perversion and even murder (see Rom 1:29). Just like we can murder someone with a gun, we must be careful not to "murder" someone with our tongue. Gossiping is a sign of a low self-image, a really bad habit or both. The best thing to do is not join in. But, when you're put in a situation where people are gossiping, you do have a few options:

1. Walk away.

2. Tell your friends that gossiping is wrong and refer to the old adage, "If you can't say something nice, don't say anything at all."

3. Turn the conversation around by either saying something positive or by changing the subject.

Words are very powerful and our tongues are hypocritical. James 3:9 says, "With the tongue we praise our Lord and Father, and with it we curse men, who have been made in God's likeness." Ephesians 4:29 tells us to say things that are "helpful for building others up according to their needs, that it may benefit those who listen." Your positive example will be the best way to keep your friends from gossiping.

55. I Am Worried About My Friend's Smoking

My friend used to smoke heavily. She quit for a year, but recently became a "social smoker" because another friend she met smokes. She tries to hide it and often lies about her smoking. I'm very against smoking and don't know what to do.

I appreciate your love and care for your friend. I'm sorry your friend is smoking again, but I'm glad you didn't say "my ex-friend." She probably needs you now more than ever before. Our job as Christians is to love people despite their habits and pitfalls. I'm afraid too many Christians walk away from their friends at the first sign of a negative outward behavior. I'm glad you aren't doing that.

Here's the scoop on smoking. Nicotine is one of the strongest addictive drugs known. Some experts say it's easier to get off heroin than nicotine. Your friend is putting a very addictive and harmful substance into her body. Some students use tobacco as a symbol of rebellion. What they don't realize is that nicotine produces a stimulating effect, causing addiction to take place quite rapidly. Once they are addicted, the withdrawal process is extremely difficult. You say your friend is a "social smoker," but she may be smoking much more than she says. Addicts tend to lie about their amount of use.

Tell your friend you still want to be friends even if she doesn't quit smoking. Also, tell her you'll help her do anything to quit. Pray for her. Be there for her and when she looks for help, she will look to you.

56. Can't I Smoke and Be a Christian?

I've been a Christian for a while now, and I love God with all my heart, but I smoke. I've tried to quit, but I always start back up again. In some ways, it's gotten in the way of my relationship with God because I feel guilty about it. But in another way, I don't see why this should affect my faith. It doesn't really make me any less of a Christian. There are a lot worse things I could be doing, like drinking or having sex. I guess I'm not sure why smoking is such a big deal.

You're right, there are "worse" things you could be doing. And it's very true that God loves you unconditionally, not for what you do, but for who you are.

Now that we have those points out of the way, let's talk about your addiction to nicotine. Maybe you don't think of yourself as an addict, but you are. Nicotine, the drug in cigarettes, is one of the most addictive drugs there is. You know its power because you've tried to stop, and, as you found out, it isn't easy. Here are four reasons why I hope you will do whatever it takes to quit smoking:

Reason #1: Cigarettes can eventually kill you. As a smoker, you're much more at risk for lung cancer and heart disease, to mention only two of the ways you could die from your addiction to nicotine. When companies place warnings on the cigarette packages you buy, they do it for a reason. Cigarette smoking has been proven to be very harmful. Can you be a Christian and smoke? Yes. Will you quite possibly die earlier and lead a less healthy life? Yes.

Reason #2: Nicotine is a "gateway drug." You've probably heard this term in school. It simply means that, because you smoke, there is a greater chance that you'll also begin to use other harmful drugs.

Reason #3: It may be illegal. I don't know how old you are, but if you're under 18, it's against the law for you to smoke. And as Christians, we are supposed to obey the law (see Heb 13:17).

Reason #4: Your body is the temple of God (see 1 Cor 6:19). This means you are to strive to keep your body pure and stay away from anything that would harm you or keep you from God. That includes all kinds of things, like drinking, premarital sex, overeating, starving yourself, drug abuse, self-mutilation and smoking.

My mother started smoking at age fifteen. She would probably beg you to quit now, before the addiction becomes even more intense. But she isn't able to do that. She died a terrible death from lung cancer a few years ago. For your family's sake, your future spouse and children's sake, for your faith's sake and for your own quality of life, do the right thing and quit your nicotine habit today. Throw those cigarettes away. Then tell a friend about your decision, and ask that friend to hold you accountable and keep you from ever lighting up again.

57. My Friend Is Smoking Pot

A good friend of mine recently started smoking pot. She shows up at school really out of it. She says she wants to try even stronger drugs. I'm scared for her, but I don't know how to help her. She's not a Christian, so I can't tell her to talk to my youth pastor. What can I say or do to get her to stop?

Your friend is gambling with her life more than she may even realize. Thank you for your concern for her. I hope you will continue to show her kindness and friendship by your actions and words of concern.

Tell her you're worried about her. Let her know you'd be glad to listen if she ever wants to talk about her problem. Tell her you know others, like your school counselor, who are also willing to help out. Just knowing you're there for her may be all she needs to turn to you for help—when she's ready.

Your friend probably doesn't fully understand the major dangers of smoking pot. Let me mention just a few. Marijuana is a drug. It alters your mood and your senses. This means that when you use pot, you become intoxicated, or high, much like you would with alcohol. When people are high, they don't have full control of their emotions or other senses. That loss of control can lead to car accidents, unplanned pregnancies, even death. Marijuana also produces what experts call "Amotivational Syndrome." This means your brain can actually slow down and become lethargic or lazy, like it does when you're very tired. Sometimes, this damage is permanent and irreversible. Like I said, your friend is headed for real trouble.

Most teenagers don't realize that the marijuana used today is much stronger than the stuff used in the 1960s. This means your friend's high is different and stronger than the high teens were getting thirty years ago. Lastly, marijuana is what we call a "gateway" drug. This means there is a good chance your friend will move on to harder drugs, like cocaine, heroin and Ecstasy.

Your friend needs to know this information. But she may not care that she's getting herself into some real trouble. So while you can give her the facts, what your friend needs most is your positive encouragement and your prayers. Remember, only God can turn a life around.

58. My Friend Is on Drugs

I've been friends with this guy for about eight months, and even though we don't have much in common, we get along well. But he's on drugs. What should I do? How can I get him to stop?

Your friend needs help. A drug addict must get off the drugs or their life will just get worse. People often take drugs to deaden pain. If your friend is stressed about school or is having family problems, drugs ease his pain, but only temporarily. If anything, drugs can make it worse.

Drug users often forget how to cope with stress. They often move rapidly from the experimental stage to complete dependency. Drugs are scary and dangerous. At first, they may make you feel good, but when it leads to addiction, addicts must get help or they'll have problems all their life. Your friend is fortunate to have a friend like you who cares so much about him.

Confront your friend. Find a place where he can turn for help in kicking his habit. Find former drug addicts who are now clean; they could have a powerful impact on your friend. Pray for him; God can help make him whole again. Ask your youth pastor or pastor for help and suggestions. Your friend is in much more trouble than he may think if he doesn't do something about his drug problem.

59. Why Did My Friend Die?

A good friend of mine died a few months ago. I've been really depressed and still have a broken heart. Why would God let bad stuff happen to us if he loves us so much?

Your letter brought back the hurt of when my best friend died. It's still painful. Here's how I've been coping with it.

Life is a gift. You and I had absolutely no input on when or if we'd be born. And we also don't know when we'll die. God gives us the gift of life and in his plan, everyone dies. Focusing on what I like to call the "eternal perspective" helps me a great deal. If your friend was a Christian, you can take comfort in knowing he or she has been transitioned from this life on earth to his or her eternal home with God. Here's what the Bible says about heaven: "He will wipe every tear from their eyes. There will be no more death or mourning or crying or pain, for the old order of things has passed away" (Rv 21:4). As much as you want your friend here on earth, you can still find comfort and hope because you know your friend is in a better place.

If your friend wasn't a Christian, you unfortunately won't find much comfort in that eternal perspective. Frankly, it's harder to deal with the death of a non-Christian friend because we can't say they've "gone to a better place." But one positive thing can result from the death of a non-Christian friend: It can encourage us to be more determined to share our faith with nonbelievers, so we can know that they also will have eternal life with God.

Regardless of whether your friend was a Christian or not, you'll want to talk with your youth worker or pastor about your question. Please know it's OK to share your pain, doubts, questions and even anger with God. You also used the words "really depressed" to describe your feelings. If you're still feeling that way now, you should see a professional counselor.

Finally, you didn't mention whether you're feeling suicidal, but if you are, I urge you not to take your own life. Seek help *immediately*. Tell someone right away. Suicide replaces a temporary problem with a permanent tragedy. Hold on. If you don't have anyone to talk to, call 9-1-1 and explain your situation. Or call 1-800-SUICIDE, 1-800-NEW-LIFE or 1-800-383-HOPE.

Before my friend Rob died, I got on my knees and begged God to heal him. For a few months I even thought he would recover, but then he died. I had prayed and even tried to get God to see things my way. "Rob is a good man. He's still needed by his three teenage children and his beautiful wife. Rob is making a difference for your kingdom." When I was at the memorial service I seemed to hear a still, small voice inside me saying, "I love Rob more than you can imagine. I allow bad things to happen. You will have to trust me on this. However, through your pain, please don't ever forget what I've promised through Scripture: 'I will never leave you nor forsake you' (Heb 13:5, NKJV). I have never said I would keep you or your loved ones free from pain and even death. However, I did promise that I would walk with you through your difficult circumstances."

60. Why Wouldn't God Save Him?

One of my best friends died after fighting cancer for a year. He was a strong Christian and only fifteen. I grew up hearing that God is loving and that as long as we trust God, everything will be OK. But now that seems so lame. I know God didn't cause my friend to die, but I just can't understand why he had to suffer the way he did. Doesn't God care?

I believe the Bible shows us God really does care. Jesus shed tears at the death of his friend Lazarus. In the Old Testament, we see God expressing righteous anger when his people are treated unjustly. God's commitment to us is so strong that he sacrificed his only Son so that the world might be saved. Yes, it's quite clear God cares.

But your question is one most of us have had at one time or another. Where is God in the midst of tragedies? What went wrong when a very bad thing happened to a very good person? I wish I had a simple answer that could satisfy the questions we all have about God. But I don't. Why a committed young Christian suffers and dies of cancer while a drug dealer who preys on children lives to old age is not for me to answer or understand. That's just one of the many issues of living in a less-than-perfect world that's awfully hard to figure out.

However, I'm not sure I completely agree with your statement, "As long as we trust God, everything will be OK." The Bible is quite clear that God will walk with us through life's problems, and that he will never leave us or forsake us (see Dt 31:8; Heb 13:5). But he never promises a life free from pain or suffering. Throughout the Bible, the people who trusted God most were also the people who suffered the most. Look at Job or the apostle Paul. They each suffered greatly. But they held on to their faith because they understood something important: God's ways are different from our ways. What seems best to us is not always what's best to God.

When my mom was dying of cancer, I couldn't say "Praise the Lord! My mom is going to be with God!" I prayed for her healing and hoped God would keep this good woman around for several more years. Yet, when she died, I was faced with the truth that Mom is happier today in heaven than she would have been on earth. If I truly wanted the best for Mom, then I needed to trust that God's way was the best, even though it wasn't the best for me.

I know it doesn't take away your pain, but I hope it's comforting to know your friend is at this very moment happier than you or I can even imagine. He is in a place where there is no sorrow or sickness. He is living in the presence of God.

We may have to wait until we join God in heaven to get some of our questions answered. Until then, take a look at Psalm 23. It reminds us that God may not always take away our suffering, but he will always walk beside us, leading us toward the best future possible—an eternal life with him.

61. There Is So Much Pain

Four of my friends were killed in a car accident, and I'm not sure how to deal with it. They were all Christians, so I know they're in heaven. But that doesn't seem to help. I can't talk about my feelings with my other friends because they're in as much pain as I am and can't help. My youth leaders are doing their best, but it's still so hard. How can I get through this? Will I ever get through it?

Yes, you will get through this tragedy. Even so, you will probably always feel a loss when you think about those friends. We experience a great deal of pain when tragedy comes our way. Getting over it isn't easy. But with the Lord's help, the scar in your heart will heal.

Please talk to someone about your pain. Don't feel that you are a burden to your youth workers or anyone else. When my mom died, I didn't need people to give me canned answers. I just needed people who would listen to me when I felt like talking and give me a hug. It's critical that you find others to help you in your grief, whether it's your youth leaders, your parents, other friends or your pastor.

Finally, I love this promise from the mouth of Jesus: "Come to me, all you who are weary and burdened, and I will give you rest" (Mt 11:28). God is not afraid of tragedy. He lives in the midst of our pain. Look to Jesus and Christian brothers and sisters to be your strength.

62. I've Started Cutting Myself

I sometimes hurt myself intentionally. I've cut myself with a razor blade and burned a heart onto my leg. I don't think I'm psycho or anything, but I'm not sure why I do it. My boyfriend broke up with me because of this. Is there something wrong with me?

Thanks for writing. Let me be blunt: Cutting your body is not a good thing. Intentionally hurting yourself in any way is not a good thing. Burning your leg and cutting yourself are extremely dangerous acts. These things suggest there's something going on inside you that even you might not understand. I urge you to seek out a Christian counselor. Ask your pastor or a school counselor to help you find a local counselor (you don't have to go into detail, just tell them you'd like to talk to someone), or call a hotline like 1-800-Hit-Home to find a counselor in your area.

In addition to counseling, you need the support of a mature friend or two. Find a trusted adult whom you can call when you feel the urge to cut or burn yourself. Ask this person to hold you accountable, to talk with you until the urge passes. And if there's ever a time when you can't find anyone to talk to, please go to the emergency room of your local hospital and talk with someone there.

In my experience with others who've intentionally hurt themselves, I've found there's often some unresolved anger lurking beneath the surface. That anger is often directed at oneself and is manifested as self-abuse. You're dealing with something very serious. The fact that you're writing to me tells me you really want to stop hurting yourself. I think you can get past this, but you need the help of a professional.

63. Are Tattoos and Body Piercing Wrong?

What does the Bible say about body piercing and tattoos? Would it be wrong to get a tattoo even if it's something as innocent as a ladybug?

You have raised a very controversial topic. The Bible really doesn't speak directly about piercing or tattooing, but both have become very popular today. Many people will choose to pierce and tattoo. When you are an adult, what you decide is really between you and God. However, my wife and I have chosen not to allow our own teenagers to get anything more than their ears pierced while they live in our home. And they aren't allowed to get a tattoo—even if it is just a ladybug. But we have good reasons behind our rules. Sometimes teenagers, and adults too for that matter, make decisions they regret. Occasionally, my job as a parent is to delay the decision until adulthood. Recently, my family was looking through my junior high and high school yearbooks. We spent more time laughing at the hairstyles and clothing then anything else in the books. I must admit that what I thought was cool when I was sixteen now looks awful.

We can change our hairstyle and our clothes, but a tattoo is permanent! Today you like ladybugs, but what about ten years from now when ladybugs are out or the tattoo phase of your life is over? The decisions you make today will affect you for the rest of your life.

Before you decide to permanently mark your body with piercings or tattoos, ask yourself the following questions:

What statement am I making with this piercing or tattoo?

Does it honor God? How might this decision affect me ten years from now? Twenty? Thirty?

Once you have answered these questions, get the opinion of your parents and pastor. They might not always be right, but it is wise to seek the counsel of others before making a permanent decision.

64. My Friend Is Into Witchcraft

What do you think about witchcraft? My friend says she only uses it for good, but in my opinion, all witchcraft is wrong. I told her it's a bad idea to mess with things we only "think" we have control over. Besides that warning, I don't have much to say to her. I'm not very familiar with witchcraft, so I don't know what Christ would say. But I want to do more than pray for my friend. How can I help her?

Let me start by saying I believe your concerns about your friend are justified. When students flirt with witchcraft, I believe they are flirting with significant spiritual forces. But I don't think most people who check out witchcraft go into it with evil intentions. They enter into it somewhat innocently.

Then they get progressively more involved, in much the same way people become addicted to drugs: They start with simple experimentation but are drawn into a much stronger and deeper connection to evil. Without early intervention, even a slight fascination with occult practices, like witchcraft, can become an all-consuming obsession.

How can you help your friend? Introduce her to the true source of her search for meaning, the Lord of Light. No matter how crazy your friend's beliefs may seem, or how antagonistic she is toward Christianity, you share at least one interest already—you're both looking for real spirituality, for beliefs that can change your life. The problem is, she's looking in all the wrong places.

Satan doesn't want your friend to find real spirituality through faith in Christ. The Bible calls him the "Father of Lies" for good reason. Satan is very deceptive, making spiritual darkness look like spiritual light. I think that's one reason people like your friend can experiment with witchcraft and not understand what they're getting into. They can truly believe practicing witchcraft is good.

But witchcraft is far from good. In 2 Chronicles 33:6, we clearly see that sorcery and witchcraft are evil in God's eyes. So I encourage you to do what you can to help your friend.

One great way you can help her see Jesus is by continuing to be her friend. You can't simply count on her interest in witchcraft to fade away, although it might, but you can patiently urge her toward the Light. You can do this by demonstrating God's unconditional love. Get together regularly to hang out, hit a movie or go for a walk. Invite her to youth group or church. Be a person she can count on for a listening ear and solid advice.

I have one very important caution, though. Don't allow yourself to be drawn into any of her witchcraft rituals or literature. As a Christian influence in her life, you should be willing to talk to her about witchcraft. Yet always be clear on your stance against the occult. I would also encourage you to see if your friend would talk to your pastor or youth pastor about witchcraft. Getting help from a wise Christian adult may not only help your friend, but it can also help solidify your own thinking about ideas contrary to your beliefs.

Finally, it's essential to understand there is a spiritual battle going on all around us. Here is the way Ephesians 6:12 explains it: "For our struggle is not against flesh and blood, but against the rulers, against the authorities, against the powers of this dark world and against the spiritual forces of evil in the heavenly realms." One of the best ways to fight this battle is through prayer (see Eph 6:18).

I have seen miracles happen when friends and parents pray for a person involved in witchcraft. In prayer, you'll find the strength to continue the relationship with your friend. Be sure to pray that God will protect your friend. Pray for your own strength to be the kind of person she needs. And pray that God will give her the will and ability to fight against the forces of evil.

65. I've Become an Abuser

I have a very scary problem. I was sexually and emotionally abused as a child. But that doesn't bother me much anymore. What really bothers me is that I've become an abuser. I hit my sister a lot. I've

hit most of my friends, too. I don't want to hurt anyone, but this rage just grabs me and I start to hit people. It scares me! I never want to date or get married because I'm afraid I'll kill someone. I'm a Christian, and I know I shouldn't be this way. I can't afford counseling, and I don't know what to do.

First, let me say I appreciate your honesty and vulnerability. Because you are willing to openly share your problem, I believe you can receive the help you need. And you do need to get help. Your history of abuse, both as a victim and now as the person lashing out at others, is not something you can get over all alone. You need the support and guidance of a professional Christian counselor.

As I read your letter, I got an image in my head of a can of soda. If you've ever shaken up a carbonated soda can, you know what happens when you open the can—it explodes! The rage you feel is like that shaken-up soda. It's trapped inside you, waiting to explode in a violent outburst. Until you get the help you need, you'll probably continue to express your rage through violence. A professional can help you find more appropriate ways to deal with your anger.

You mentioned that you don't have the money for a counselor. Please don't let a lack of money keep you from getting the help you desperately need. Go to your pastor or a school counselor and tell them what you have told me. If you don't feel comfortable talking to someone in person, call 1-800-NEW-LIFE. They can help you find inexpensive or even free counseling in your area. And if you're still dependent on your parents, their medical insurance policy might include coverage for counseling. If you are able to discuss this situation with your parents, ask them what's available.

It seems clear to me that the trauma of the emotional and sexual abuse you experienced as a child is a major part of the rage you feel today. Everyone who suffers from abuse deals with it differently. Your way of dealing with the abuse is rage. That's a common reaction. Something awful happened to you. And it's important for you to know that the abuse that took place in your life was definitely not your fault. It was the fault of the abuser.

But you *are* responsible for how you handle the pain and anger you feel. Abuse can do so much damage to a person that it can be hard to think straight and find a way out of all that rage. This is why you need professional help. You need to find healing from your own pain before you can stop causing pain to others.

I also want you to find a Christian adult you can trust— someone with whom you can be brutally honest about your feelings. It might be your parents, your youth pastor, another adult at your church, a relative or the parent of a friend. Tell this person what's going on in your life. Ask this person to be available for you to call when you feel the rage coming on. Meet with this person regularly to read the Bible and pray. Ask him or her to help you stick with your professional counseling. You'll need the love and support of a mature Christian as you work toward healing and recovery.

When I was in graduate school, I was a chaplain in a prison. Every week I would meet prisoners who were locked up because of some crime of rage. Many of these people had been abused when they were younger and never sought help. They didn't know how to handle their rage, so they lashed out at others. During that same time in my life, I was also working with a youth group. I'd talked to students there who had struggled with abuse, yet had chosen to deal with their pain in a healthy manner. These students had decided to seek God's help and the help of a professional. I hope you follow their example. With honesty and a willingness to seek counsel, you can make it.

66. My Friend Is Gay

I recently faced a dilemma: A friend of mine has come out of the closet about being a homosexual. He says he's been gay since he was twelve, and now he's almost eighteen. Although my friend became a Christian five months ago, it hasn't changed his sexual orientation. My problem is, I don't know how to approach him in a kind, loving manner and tell him what the Bible says about homosexuality. What can I do?

You do have a difficult dilemma. Homosexuality is a very complicated and misunderstood issue. We, as Christians, have not done a very good job of presenting biblical truth in a kind, loving manner. Many Christians have either made fun of homosexuals or have been mean to them. Neither of these methods will ever bring the love of God to anyone.

The dilemma we have lies in the fact that the Bible is quite clear in regard to sexual sin. And that's any sexual sin—not just homosexuality. It's interesting that there are at least seventeen references to different types of sexual sin in the Bible, and only three (or at most five, depending on your interpretation) of those references deal with homosexuality.

So, according to the Bible, there is no big difference between the sin of homosexuality and any other sexual sin—premarital sex, for instance. The word "sin" in Greek, the language the New Testament was written in, literally means to "miss the mark." And all sexual sin is missing the mark of God's standards.

From my experience, I'd guess about 10 percent of the youth population has struggled with what we call gender identity confusion. Your friend is not alone in his struggles. However, I am also convinced that most people who believe they are homosexual are not. Let me give you some important information on homosexuality.

Sexual abuse is a key factor in homosexuality. Studies show that as many as 58 percent of homosexuals have experienced some kind of sexual abuse as children. Many others who call themselves homosexual were either physically or emotionally abused. Also, many homosexuals suffer from sexual addiction. With the ease of obtaining pornographic materials from the Internet, videos and magazines, some people experiment with homosexual behavior because of what they've seen and read.

A lot of Christians, including myself, believe that homosexual behaviors are preventable and treatable. Many people who experiment with homosexual behaviors are simply confused. Although the issues can be complicated, young people who struggle with homosexuality can move on to a healthy heterosexual marriage with the help of good Christian counseling.

I would also ask your friend to check out Exodus International, a Christian organization committed to helping free people from a homosexual lifestyle (www.exodusintl.org).

From my own experience talking with students, I would guess that your friend has a great deal of sexual identity confusion. Since your friend has recently become a Christian, I think that if he wants to, he will be able to seek the truth about his sexuality and receive the help he needs. Your job is to do what you said you could do: Be kind and loving, yet share your understanding of Scripture.

One thing we know about those who struggle with this issue is, the earlier they can get help, the easier it is to live a lifestyle that is glorifying to God. Please know it is never too late to get help and never too early to make wise and godly decisions about our sexuality. I commend you for caring for your friend in such a sensitive way.

67. I Have a Bad Reputation

My reputation is so bad that my pastor and youth pastor have a hard time believing I actually had a deep spiritual conversion. I want to change my life, but it's hard. And it seems that every step I take, I take two steps back. I always get pulled back down. I don't know who to look to for help. How can I change?

There is an incredibly encouraging story in the Bible about Jesus meeting someone with a bad reputation. In fact, this was a woman who'd been caught in the act of adultery. After she got caught, someone brought her to Jesus and a crowd of people so she could be punished in public. Jewish law said that as her punishment, she had to stand still while others threw stones at her. The stones would keep coming until the woman died.

But Jesus looked out at the crowd and said, "If anyone of you is without sin, let him be the first to throw a stone at her." Everyone dropped the stones they were holding and left. Jesus looked that woman in the eyes and asked her, "Woman, where are [your accusers]? Has no one condemned you?" She answered, "No one, sir."

Then Jesus said something that affects each one of us. With a great deal of compassion and love, Jesus said, "Then neither do I condemn you. Go now and leave your life of sin." This story, from John 8:1-11, is one of the greatest examples of the forgiveness Christ offers us.

I don't know what kind of conversion experience you had, but I hope it involved a real understanding of what it means to follow Christ. Just like the woman in the story, you've been confronted with God's love and mercy, and now you must decide what you'll do about it. You can repent and live for God, or you can continue to make unwise decisions. As you choose the path your life will take, here are a few things to keep in mind:

Change can only come from God. It's a good thing that true change comes from God, not from our own willpower. We are often too weak to change, but God's power combined with your willingness can equal miraculous change. So make sure you stay plugged in to him through daily prayer, time spent reading the Bible and fellowship with other Christians.

Change takes accountability and counsel. I find that when I make a decision to change my behavior, it helps to tell someone about my decision. Talk with your pastor, youth pastor or a spiritual leader in your life and tell them about your desire to grow spiritually. Ask them if you can check in with them at least once a week and talk honestly about your successes as well as your struggles. It can be a weekly phone call or even a thirty-second conversation at church. Even though your pastors are having a hard time taking your conversion seriously, they may change their minds if you're sincere about wanting to change and you show them you're willing to work at it.

Change takes discipline. I like the advice the apostle Paul gave to his disciple Timothy when he said, "Train yourself to be godly" (1 Tm 4:7). As you develop the basic practices of your faith (prayer, Bible reading, fellowship), you'll see the reversal of your "one step forward and two steps back" pattern. Pretty soon I think you'll find yourself making a habit of living in a way that honors God.

68. My Friend Is Stealing

A few months ago, I found out my best friend was stealing. Not just from stores, but from me and my friends, too. My friends and I told her how we felt. She seemed really sorry, and for awhile, she stopped. Then, just a few days ago, she confessed that she'd stolen a shirt from me a few weeks earlier. I think she's a kleptomaniac. I've prayed and I've talked to her about it, but I can't trust her anymore. We've been friends since first grade and I don't want to lose her as my friend. What can I do?

There are several reasons why your friend may be stealing. Authorities on the subject say compulsive stealing is often a result of a person's poor self-image. It sounds like your friend definitely has a serious problem that's larger than anything you can fix on your own. Your friend needs the help of a professional Christian counselor who can help her overcome her compulsion to steal. With that in mind, I want to focus on your concerns about keeping her as a friend.

Yes, she has a problem. But the fact that she was honest enough to admit that she stole from you offers a little bit of hope for both of you. She obviously wants to keep your friendship. And for now, that's enough to go on. This may sound crazy, but I don't think you have to trust her to remain her friend. Sure, there must be some basic trust, but you don't have to give her your full trust. You can show her care and friendship even though you don't have complete trust in her. In some ways, this will be a one-sided friendship. You may end up doing more giving than getting for awhile. Until she gets help and stops stealing, you can fill your need for trustworthy friends in other relationships.

She clearly trusts you. She knows you're the kind of friend she needs to help her get over this problem. If she didn't feel that way, I doubt she'd have listened to the concerns you and your other friends expressed. I doubt she would have told you about stealing your shirt. And I doubt she'd still be interested in having any kind of friendship with you. So she wants to hold on to your friendship.

With this in mind, I encourage you to tell her that trust is an important part of a healthy friendship, the kind you want with her. Tell her how much you care about her and that you value the friendship you share. Let her know that her efforts to be honest about her problem are good steps toward earning your trust. No one is perfect, so assure her that's not what you expect from her. But help her see that her stealing is unacceptable. Encourage her to keep on working to overcome this obvious problem in her life. If she's open to seeking the professional help she needs, do what you can to help her find it. Offer to pray with her, and let her know you're praying for her on your own. Help her build other solid friendships with Christians who can do the same.

You have plenty of reasons to end your friendship with this girl, but it sounds like you want to keep it. Good for you. You don't have to tolerate your friend's stealing, but you can show her compassion. When your friend experiences true grace, it might cause her to get rid of this sin in her life. Hang in there with your friend, if you can, and you may just help her change her lifestyle of stealing. The combination of God's help, possibly the help of a professional, and your friendship may be the keys for your friend to choose the better road.

69. I'm Moving!

I'm transferring to a new school and I'm terrified. I'm shy and it's hard for me to make friends. I'm talkative around people I know, but around new people, I clam up and can't think of a thing to say. How can I be better at talking to people?

Making new friends can be awfully intimidating. But you don't have to do all the work. People like to talk about themselves.

So when you meet someone new, ask questions about them, what they like to do, what they're involved in. You can learn a lot about them and chances are they'll appreciate your genuine interest. Moving to a new school isn't easy. But as difficult as it is and as much as you'll want to keep to yourself, force yourself to get involved in new activities where you can meet new friends.

If you're moving to a new community, one of the first things to do is find a good church youth group, or a Christian club or Bible study at your school. They'll be natural places to develop relationships and help you get acquainted with new friends. You may also want to join a group at school that involves one of your interests, like a sports team or music group. Common interests are always great conversation starters.

I'm an extrovert and my wife Cathy is an introvert. She often feels the same way you do when faced with meeting new people. But to be honest, Cathy is a better conversationalist than I am. Introverts are awesome because they're often better listeners than those of us who want to talk all the time. And I think people like you and Cathy sometimes develop deeper relationships because of your quietness. For example, Cathy and I were recently at a party. I had shallow conversations with everyone at the party. Cathy sat in the corner of a living room with a few friends and had a very deep and meaningful conversation.

If you've got the gift of being a good listener, use it to your advantage. As you make friends at your new school, you'll find people will deeply appreciate your ability to listen, and they'll look forward to getting to know you better through the process.

70. I Like Mainstream Media

I'm a student at a very conservative Christian high school, but I don't really fit in there. The problem is, I'm really into the arts. But the people at my school act like movies and music (even contemporary Christian music) are evil. What's ironic is that I'm a very strong Christian with solid morals. My dad's a pastor. I don't swear, drink, use drugs or have sex. I read my Bible every day. I guess I just don't understand why some Christians think the arts are so sinful.

I love and appreciate the arts, too. It's always a pleasure to see and hear people expressing the creative gifts God's given them. But I'm sure you'd agree that in the midst of all the wonderful expressions of creativity out there, there's also some real trash.

That's why some Christians have a hard time supporting the arts. For them, the bad outweighs the good. They feel it's better to avoid art altogether, rather than risk being influenced by art that doesn't glorify God. And that's why all Christians need to make wise decisions when it comes to the arts.

While I don't know you, or know much about the movies and music you're choosing, it does sound like you're doing your best to make wise choices. You seem to be living your life for the Lord. Your devotional life and your choice of a healthy, Christ-centered lifestyle are evidence that you are striving to be all that God wants you to be.

But to make sure you aren't compromising your faith in any way, I'd suggest you talk to some people who do know you well. Talk to your parents and other Christian leaders you respect. Let them hear the music you're listening to. Tell them about the movies you like. Get their opinions and seek their counsel.

I'd also encourage you to keep Philippians 4:8 in mind. Paul's got some sound advice to help us determine what kinds of interests we ought to pursue. He says, "Whatever is true, whatever is noble, whatever is right, whatever is pure, whatever is lovely, whatever is admirable—if anything is excellent or praiseworthy—think about such things." I hope you will continue to pursue your love for the arts. As you do, I hope you'll seek the advice of Christian role models and continue listening to the Holy Spirit who dwells within you.

71. I'm Uncomfortable With Evolution

I go to a public school and in our science classes we learn about the theory of evolution. I feel uncomfortable when my teachers try to tell me I evolved from a gorilla. How do I handle situations like this?

I had a similar problem with one of my college classes. I remember the frustrations I had, but going back to study what I believed helped me through. You, too, have to make a choice on how you're going to handle this situation. You have a couple options. You can take science as a home school course, while continuing to take other classes at your public school. Or, you can look for a different teacher in your school who shares your beliefs and ask to be switched to that class.

However, don't consider any of these options without seriously thinking about staying in the class and studying twice as hard as you need to for the grade. I've seen students who read their text, listen to lectures and then study books that support a different view. They also spend time talking with pastors about Creation. You can also try to argue with the science teacher, but my experience says that usually doesn't work as well as investing the extra time to study both sides and come up with a well thought-out belief of your own. The important thing in this situation is to explore the theories of evolution and Creation for yourself so you may be confident in God and your belief in him.

72. Am I Sinning?

Is saying "Oh my God" a sin? I say that, and I can't kick the habit.

Whenever you're in a crowd and you hear someone call your name, don't you turn around to see if they're talking to you? Of course you do. The same goes for God. When someone says, "Oh my God," they're calling on the name of their Creator.

The Bible clearly tells us not to take the name of God in vain. The Ten Commandments say, "You shall not misuse the name of the Lord your God" (Ex 20:7).

Do you mean to abuse the name of God when you use that popular phrase? Probably not. But whenever we say the name of God, we are calling upon him to listen to us and respond to our prayer.

When we say "Oh my God" as an expression of surprise, we've cheapened the name of our Creator. Using his name in a casual manner trivializes our relationship with God. In the Old Testament, one of the names for God is Yahweh. This name was so special to the Hebrew people that they would only whisper it. The Jews felt God's name was so holy they wouldn't even personalize it.

Christians have a personal relationship with God only because of our relationship with Jesus. But we are still called to respect the name of God and hold it in reverence. Far too many people say "Oh my God." Do everything you can to kick the habit.

73. Four-Letter Words Are Just Words

Is it really a sin to cuss? I know saying the Lord's name in vain is wrong, but what's the big deal with four-letter words? As far as I know, the Bible doesn't say anything about them. They're just words, so why is it wrong to say them?

Your letter reminded me of something that happened to me when my children were young. I took two of them to a movie. As we were waiting for the show to start, we couldn't help but overhear some high-school students sitting near us. Their conversation was filled with vile cuss words. I'll admit my first emotion was anger—not because I'd never heard those words, but because I felt their language was totally inappropriate in the presence of children. In my opinion, it cheapened the integrity of those teenagers, making them look rude and disrespectful.

You asked if cussing is a sin. The Bible actually does say something about the words we use:

Do not let any unwholesome talk come out of your mouths.

EPHESIANS 4:29

If anyone considers himself religious and yet does not keep a tight rein on his tongue, he deceives himself and his religion is worthless.

JAMES 1:26

I won't tell you that a four-letter word has never come from my own lips. I'm not going to tell you that as a junior-high student I didn't have a vocabulary that makes me shudder now. But I believe the use of four-letter words does nothing, and I mean nothing, to help my relationship with God. And using cuss words certainly doesn't reflect God to other people. So my goal is to try my best to keep those words from my lips and substitute them with a better choice of vocabulary. There are so many words we can use to express ourselves, to communicate with other people. Why cuss when it only cheapens the meaning of what you really want to say?

FIVE

Spiritual Life

74. I Feel Far From God

Lately my personal relationship with Christ has deteriorated, almost to the point of nonexistence. I've tried praying but it hasn't been working. I'm lost and have no idea how to become close to him again.

I wish I had a specific formula to help you find your way back to God. But the truth is there just isn't one. However, there is a wonderful Scripture I hope you'll see as a great promise: "Come near to God and he will come near to you" (Jas 4:8). And how do you draw near to God? Well, some people find that prayer draws them back to God. Others revive their relationship with Christ through serving or through a mission trip. I know a person who went camping and while sitting by a lake, surrounded by mountains, felt God's presence. And then there's Kara, a teen with the same problem as yours, who said getting involved in a small group at her church helped. It was when she started hanging out with strong Christians that her faith became real to her. Again, I must stress that I am not offering a "magic formula" for renewing your faith. I am simply pointing out that God can use a lot of different situations and circumstances to draw people back to himself.

I also want to encourage you not to put too much faith in

your feelings. We can't always trust our feelings, because they come and go. But God never changes. He loves you always, and nothing can stop that—not your feelings, not anything (Rom 8:35-39).

I don't know your specific situation, but when I was in college I struggled with the same thing. I wanted to be closer to God, but felt so far away. One verse in the book of John turned me in the right direction. "Whoever has my commands and obeys them, he is the one who loves me. He who loves me will be loved by my Father, and I too will love him and show myself to him" (Jn 14:21). Here's the principle I learned from those words of Jesus: No matter what I *feel* about God, my job is to obey him. When I obey and follow him, it shows him that I love him and in return, he promises to reveal himself to me.

Soon after learning the verse, I decided to end a friendship that was having a negative effect on me and went on a mission trip to Mexico. Both acts of obedience helped me get back on the right path and sense God's presence in my life. When you are quiet before God, when you look deep into your soul, what is it that you believe God is whispering to you? Obey his whisper and come back to him. He will do the rest.

75. How Do I Keep My Faith Strong?

I spent a week at a Bible camp this summer and had a blast! But now I'm home and I just don't feel like I can keep my faith strong without my camp friends. How can I keep the excitement for God I had at camp?

It's easy to get excited about God and feel unbelievably close to him at camp. When you mix the intense times with God with a whole lot of fun, you get a lifelong, positive memory. And that's why a lot of people find it hard to come down off that camp "high."

By its very design, camp is a "mountaintop experience." It's meant to be a time to jump-start your faith. The hard part is what you're experiencing now, the letdown. But the good news is that you can use what you learned during your time at camp to make your "real life" faith much stronger. I've found a way to help myself make the most of life's "mountaintop experiences." This formula helps me feel close to God, even when I've come down off that mountain. I call it the GROW plan:

Go to God daily in prayer. Most likely you prayed often at camp, so keep up the habit with a daily quiet time with God (see 1 Thes 5:17).

Read the Bible often. God's Word will reveal much of his will for your life and it will keep your faith strong (see Ps 119:105).

Obey God's Word. As you obey the Lord, you will know his presence and keep from making unwise decisions (see Jn 14:21).

Worship and serve God with other believers. Just like at camp, fellowship with other Christians is often what carries us through the hard times and encourages us to stay firm in our faith (see Ps 150:6, Heb 10:24-25).

I can't promise you'll always have the same awesome feelings you had at camp, but if you follow the GROW plan, you'll develop the kind of strong faith that can carry you through life's valleys and up to the next mountaintop.

76. I'm Ready to Give Up the Faith

I feel like God and I have a one-way relationship. I don't believe God is there for me. I want to know the loving God people talk about, but it seems impossible. I feel totally worthless in God's eyes. I've been going to counseling with my youth leader for more than a year, but it hasn't helped. I'm ready to give up on my faith. What can I do?

I appreciate your sincerity and your desire to want to know the loving God of the Bible. My hope and prayer is that you will keep pursuing the God who promises his love and commitment to you.

I'm not sure what got you to the place in your life where you feel worthless in God's eyes, but somewhere along the line, you developed a major misconception of God's love and acceptance. So the first thing I want you to do is find your Bible and read some Scripture.

The Bible speaks endlessly about God's love for his people. Here are a few verses:

> "Though the mountains be shaken and the hills be removed, yet my unfailing love for you will not be shaken nor my covenant of peace be removed," says the Lord, who has compassion on you.
>
> ISAIAH 54:10

For God so loved the world that he gave his one and only son, that whoever believes in him shall not perish but have eternal life.

JOHN 3:16

Be strong and courageous. Do not be afraid or terrified because of them, for the Lord your God goes with you; he will never leave you nor forsake you.

DEUTERONOMY 31:6

Being confident of this, that he who began a good work in you will carry it on to completion until the day of Christ Jesus.

PHILIPPIANS 1:6

And surely I am with you always, to the very end of the age.

MATTHEW 28:20

Finally, I encourage you to keep talking with your youth leader, or another Christian adult. Find a few other Christian friends with whom you can share your struggles. You might be surprised to find that many Christians feel as you do at times. I also suggest finding a way to minister to others. Do a service project. Serve lunch at a soup kitchen. Go on a mission trip. Visit a nursing home. Even when I'm feeling far away from God, I sense God's presence when I feel God working through me in the lives of other people.

77. I Can't Hear God

I really believe in the power of prayer, but I sometimes have trouble listening to God. How can I better listen for God's answers?

In order to hear God, you have to learn to recognize his voice. It's a very important part of our two-way relationship with God. Samuel, an Old Testament prophet, learned this lesson as a young boy. God spoke to him in an audible voice, but Samuel didn't know who was talking to him. Eli, a priest who was older and wiser, helped Samuel determine that he was hearing God's voice. Eli instructed him to respond, "Speak, Lord, for your servant is listening" (1 Sm 3:9).

Today, God doesn't need to speak in an audible voice. He has given us his Word, the Bible. That's the main way he communicates with us. He also uses people and circumstances. But figuring out what God is trying to say to you isn't easy. Like Samuel, you'll have to learn to recognize God's voice.

Here are a couple ways you can do this:

Make an appointment with God. Spend some time with him in a quiet place. Read his Word, sing a worship song, praise him, thank him, confess your sins to him and ask for his presence in your life.

Take time to empty your mind. Be quiet before the Lord. Bring a journal and write whatever flows through your mind. Everything you write down won't be coming from God. But the more time you spend in solitude, the more you'll be able to discipline yourself to listen to God.

Most of us don't take the time to experience silence and solitude. Jesus sets an excellent example when he "went off to a solitary place, where he prayed" (Mk 1:35). Jesus recognized listening as a part of praying. His strength came from his solitude.

We often rush through our prayer time, if we ever have it, and then are off doing whatever is next on our busy schedule. Jesus found his strength in listening to his Father. If solitude was necessary for Jesus, it seems like it should be essential for us, too.

78. God's No Fun

I have accepted Jesus into my heart several times, and each time I did, I really felt like I wanted to change my life. But when I'm outside of church, I don't feel that way anymore. I'm not ready to give up things for Jesus. I don't think I love him enough to want to change my life. I believe you should live life to the fullest, and Christianity is only concerned about life after death. I find myself wanting to give up on Christianity and just live life how I want to. Please give me some advice.

I think you might have some mixed-up messages about Christianity. Jesus told his disciples, "I have come that they may have life, and have it to the full" (Jn 10:10b). That doesn't sound to me like the Lord is only interested in life after death. Christianity is much more than the assurance of eternal life with God after we die. The best possible way to live life to the fullest is to live your life with Jesus as your master. You'll find he's not "the great killjoy." On the contrary, he wants to lead you in a life of fullness and adventure. And he will do that as you seek to obey his will. If you trust that God's plan for you is best, you'll find it's better than anything you could have come up with on your own.

You aren't alone in your struggle to give up the things of this world. The apostle Paul said this about his life:

> I have the desire to do what is good, but I cannot carry it out. For what I do is not the good I want to do; no, the evil I do not want to do—this I keep on doing. Now if I do what I do not want to do, it is no longer I who do it, but it is sin living in me that does it. So I find this law at work: When I want to do good, evil is right there with me.... What a wretched man I am! Who will rescue me from this body of death? Thanks be to God—through Jesus Christ our Lord.
>
> ROMANS 7:18b-21, 24-25

Notice that Paul answered his own dilemma when he thanked God for rescuing him and giving him eternal life through Jesus. You can do the same. Don't give up on your faith. Seek out a strong group of Christians to help you enjoy God's best for you each and every day of your life—beginning right now.

79. Has God Really Changed Me?

I asked God into my heart, but I don't feel any different. Everybody I know talks about becoming a "new person," but I still feel bad about myself. I don't feel like a new person. I asked God into my heart again, thinking I would feel different this time, but I don't. Why don't I feel like a new person?

It's very possible to be a "brand new person" in Christ and still feel many or most of the same feelings you felt before becoming a Christian. When you commit your life to Jesus Christ, a miracle takes place in your soul. He enters your life, redeems you from your sin and gives you an eternal relationship with God. The Bible says, "If you confess with your mouth, 'Jesus is Lord,' and believe in your heart that God raised him from the dead, you will be saved. For it is with your heart that you believe and are justified, and it is with your mouth that you confess and are saved" (Rom 10:9-10).

Our faith is not primarily about feelings, but about facts—including the one from the Romans verse above. Consider these other facts from the Bible:

Fact one: "Therefore, if anyone is in Christ, he is a new creation; the old has gone, the new has come!" (2 Cor 5:17)

Fact two: "Yet to all who received him, to those who believed in his name, he gave the right to become children of God" (Jn 1:12).

Fact three: "If we confess our sins, he is faithful and just and will forgive us our sins and purify us from all unrighteousness" (1 Jn 1:9).

If you accept these verses as true and you have asked Jesus into your life, then you *are* a new person. Jesus did for you exactly what these verses claimed he would. Feelings aren't very reliable. They change as often as the weather and are influenced by a number of factors. That's why it's so important to base our relationship with God on the fact of his Word and the faith that it is true.

80. I Don't Have a Testimony

I'm not sure when Jesus came into my heart. The first time I asked was when I was young, but I've done it several times since then. Isn't it important to know when you first got saved? How can I tell others about my experience if I don't even remember it? Should I just make up a date so I have a testimony to share?

I don't think it's important to know the exact date you asked Jesus into your heart as long as you know you have done it. Many wonderful Christians made their commitment to Jesus as children and have no idea what date they experienced God's redemption. God knows the date, and that's what matters!

If it's your commitment to Jesus Christ you're unsure about—and not just the date—I have a suggestion. Romans 10:9 says, "If you confess with your mouth, 'Jesus is Lord,' and believe in your heart that God raised him from the dead, you will be saved." Consider this verse, and ask yourself if it describes you. Do you understand what it's saying? I would encourage you to speak with your youth leader if you're not certain.

81. I'm Too Busy for God

I'm too busy for God! I know that sounds bad, but it's true. I take Advanced Placement classes and am involved in many extracurricular activities. These things are important to me, and they're important to my future. Does God really want me to give these things up to follow him?

I don't think God is asking a bright, enthusiastic person like yourself to quit all activities and live like a hermit. However, your first sentence, "I'm too busy for God!" does say a lot about your time commitments and priorities.

You're correct to say that things like AP classes are important to your future; when it comes time to apply to college, you'll have a good chance of being accepted at a number of fine schools. You've clearly invested a great deal of time and energy in preparing for your future, and I hope it pays off. But here's my question to you: Isn't your relationship with God also important to you and your future?

Busy people have always needed to think about their priorities. Jesus asked people to do just that with this strong and powerful statement: "Seek first his kingdom and his righteousness, and these things will be given to you as well" (Mt 6:33). In other words, Jesus is asking us to put God first and then watch as everything else falls into place. Putting God first doesn't necessarily mean giving up all your extracurricular activities and AP classes. But it does mean you need to reprioritize your life, keeping your relationship with Christ number one.

Of course, you may find you just can't make God your top

priority and still be heavily involved in all these other things. If that's the case, then I think it's time for you to pare down your involvement in extracurriculars. I'm not saying you have to drop everything, but you may need to end one or two of your commitments. To do that, make a list of everything you're involved in. Then, look at the list and rank the activities by how much you enjoy them and how well they're preparing you for the future. You might find that there are a few things you can get rid of without cutting back on your favorite activities.

You might also be surprised to know that most colleges are less impressed with the *number* of extracurricular activities than they are with your level of involvement in those activities. In other words, digging deep into the activities you really love is better than spreading yourself thin across every club, team and group you can find. Knowing this could help you decide which extracurriculars you really want to stick with and which ones you're involved in halfheartedly.

I'm not sure God wants you to give up some things *for* him as much as he wants you to give those things *to* him. The apostle Paul offers busy people some wise and challenging words about this subject: "And whatever you do, whether in word or deed, do it all in the name of the Lord Jesus, giving thanks to God the Father through him" (Col 3:17). There is nothing more exciting than people putting God first in their lives and using all their talents for him. That's why I hope you use your God-given abilities to the glory of God.

82. Who Should I Pray For?

When do you stop praying for someone? If I prayed for everyone who asked for prayer, I would have a never-ending list. When can I take them off? I know God knows our wants and needs before we go to him, but shouldn't I specifically mention people and their situations? Even if the person does change, they still need prayer so they won't fall back into their old ways. What do I do?

People handle their prayer life in different ways. I like to keep a journal. I list prayer requests and write down names. From time to time, I go back through the list and pray for people I haven't thought of for awhile. Often going back over the journal will motivate me to pray for them.

A very important part of prayer is two-way communication. In our moments of solitude, we can listen to the whisper of God. Most of the time it comes in the form of an idea or impression through our mind. During times of silence, God will often prompt a name to pray for or a situation to pray about.

I hope you will pray consistently for the people close to you. I became a Christian when I was sixteen, and I prayed for my father to make a commitment to Christ. My prayers for him were passionate and constant throughout the rest of high school and on into college. After several years, however, I prayed for him less and less. I'm not sure if I lost faith or just got lazy. But after many years God has brought me great joy because my dad recently became a Christian.

Don't give up too quickly on your prayers. God hears all of them, but he answers on *his* timing, not ours. Eventually we do get an answer from him. In 1 Thessalonians 5:17, we are commanded to "pray without ceasing" (KJV). When we pray for others, we're assured that God is watching over those we care about. I can think of no one better to take care of those we love.

83. Sign Me Up!

I've been hearing a lot lately about volunteering. I'm really interested in serving other people, but I'm not sure how to get started. I live in a pretty small town, so there aren't a lot of opportunities. How do I start volunteering?

One of the things the Bible makes very clear is that the call to Christ is the call to serve. In fact, God's command to care for the poor and oppressed is stressed throughout the Bible.

Probably the best example of service is Jesus himself. After Jesus washed his disciples' feet, he said to them, "I have set for you an example that you should do as I have done for you" (Jn 13:15). And many Christians have followed Christ's example. I love the quote by the physician Albert Schweitzer: "I don't know what your destiny will be, but one thing I know, the ones among you who will be really happy are those who have sought and found how to serve." Serving others is part of how we live out Christ's love on earth.

That's why it's great you're excited about volunteering. And living in a small town doesn't have to keep you from serving others. There are hurting people in every town who need your care and concern. Look in the Yellow Pages under "Social

Services." Call a few of the numbers you find there. If they can't use your help, they'll be able to direct you to organizations that can.

You may also want to think about your own interests, hobbies and skills and go from there. If you like working with children, volunteer to baby-sit during a church gathering. If you like to talk to people, find out how you can become a volunteer at a nursing home, where the residents are often short on visitors. Or try one of these ideas:

- Adopt a "grandparent" in your neighborhood
- Volunteer to visit sick children or other patients in the hospital
- Teach a children's Sunday school class
- Offer to work a few hours a month in the office at your church
- Tutor a child
- Help build low-income housing with an area chapter of Habitat for Humanity
- Provide free baby-sitting to a young family
- Work at an area soup kitchen or homeless shelter once a month

And remember that your volunteer opportunities aren't limited to your hometown:

- Sponsor a child through Children International (1-800-888-3089, www.children.org), World Vision (1-800-448-6437, www.worldvision.org) or Compassion International (1-800-336-7676, www.compassion.com)

- Talk to your youth pastor about short-term missions opportunities

There are endless ways to serve others. All you need to do is decide how you'd like to help, make a few calls and you're ready to go. With enthusiasm and a genuinely caring heart, your efforts can have a big impact on the lives of others.

84. I Feel Called to Missions

I'm just starting high school, but I feel a call to ministry. Actually, I've felt a call for over a year. The problem is, I don't know how to get started. Eventually, I want to be a missionary to another country, but I also want to do something now. I think my parents would support me if I had some definite plans, but I don't. What should I do?

I don't think your call is unusual or untimely. In my experience, most missionaries and pastors say they first felt God's tug on their life in their teens or earlier.

Right now, begin to develop a solid relationship with your youth leader, pastor or another full-time Christian worker you respect. Don't wait for this person to come to you—take some initiative and express your interest in a relationship. You'll learn a lot just by sharing your dreams and asking for personal insight.

You've probably got some big plans, but you'll want to start small. Find out how you can get involved in Christian ministry locally, if you aren't involved already. Consider taking a short-term mission trip; ask your youth leader for suggestions on how to arrange one. Begin corresponding with a couple of missionaries (ask your church office to help you get some addresses), and ask them about life on the mission field. And whenever missionaries visit your church, try to arrange a lunch or other meeting with them just to talk and learn.

To fuel your fire, read missionary stories. I recommend several: *Through Gates of Splendor* by Elisabeth Elliot, *Bruchko* by Bruce Olson, *Don't Let the Goats Eat the Loquat Trees* by Thomas Hale, *God's Smuggler* by Brother Andrew and *"It's a Jungle Out There!"* by Ron Snell. For other recommendations, ask your youth leader or pastor.

God has planted a dream in your heart, and that's wonderful. As time goes on, your family, friends and church will probably also confirm your call. Right now you don't need definite future plans but simply a faithful and willing heart.

85. I'm Scared to Share

I know I should be standing up for God and my beliefs at school, but for some reason I always get scared. What can I do to not be so afraid?

Many people feel the same way you do. It's not easy! I encourage you to take "baby steps." As you think about taking your faith to school, start small. Join a campus Bible study so you can meet regularly with Christians. After you take a small step in the right direction, my guess is you'll feel stronger to take a stand for God.

When Dave, a member of my youth group, became a

Christian, he was shy about sharing his faith. I encouraged him to meet and pray with one of the students in our youth group a few days a week before class. Out of that time of prayer, they decided to start a Bible study at lunch. They invited a few of their friends, and it just kept growing. By the time the year ended, sixty students were meeting at lunch for prayer and fellowship. Dave was one of the leaders and was even asked to pray at the school's graduation ceremony. This is a perfect example of a person who was as reluctant as you to bring their faith to school, yet with "baby steps" he was able to become more comfortable with showing his faith on campus.

86. The Bible Is Boring!

I'm not trying to insult the Bible, but I can't even read one chapter. I enjoy books about God, but the Bible puts me to sleep. I don't want to be this way! How can I get more interested in reading it?

You say the Bible is boring but you like to read Christian books, some of them based on the Bible. I'd guess your problem with the Bible is more centered on how you've been reading it than what's actually inside.

There are several ways you can read the Bible:

The Bible is a devotional book. You can read the Bible in bite-sized pieces, maybe with a study guide to illustrate its relevance. Since the Bible isn't just any book but the Word of God, ask him to reveal the truth of the devotional to you.

The Bible is the history of God's people. You can read the Bible as a history book, telling of God's great work.

The Bible is topical. What does it say about friendships, the end of the world, sexuality, money or even how to deal with parents? All those topics and many more are in the Bible.

The Bible is poetry. Some of the Scriptures are poems from God's people. It's wonderful to be comforted by the Psalms or given good advice from the Book of Proverbs.

The Bible is mystery. Parts of the Bible read like a novel. There are battles, love affairs, victories, defeats. There's joy, heartache, wrath, peace. All this and more.

The Bible reveals God. One way God reveals himself to us is through his Word. Although certain parts of the Bible may be more or less interesting to you, it's still the Book that God gave us to better understand his plan of eternal life.

The Bible is eternal. The prophet Isaiah says, "The grass withers and the flowers fall, but the word of our God stands forever" (Is 40:8).

Another great way to get into God's Word is to get involved in a Bible study with other Christians who are excited about it. That excitement can be contagious. Ask someone at your church to get you plugged into such a group.

Finally, you might consider another Bible translation. Some of today's Bibles are translated or paraphrased into more contemporary language that's easier to read. We recommend The New Living Translation, The Living Bible, Contemporary English Version or The Message.

Please give the Bible another try. If you read it with an open heart, I don't think it'll be as boring as you think.

SIX

Church Life

87. Our Youth Group Needs Focus

Our youth group's having problems. We used to really focus on God and his plans for us. But lately, many of the students have drifted from God. We've really lost touch with what God wants us to do. How can we get that spark back? How can we seek God and make our faith real again?

First, talk to your youth leader about the problem. He or she may be feeling the way you do, and will be glad to know you're concerned about this problem, too.

If you don't have a youth leader, talk to your senior pastor. Ask your pastor to help your group think of some adults in the church who could provide leadership. Ask those adults to prayerfully consider joining you.

Then offer to get together with other interested group members and start meeting for prayer before your regular youth group sessions. Pray for wisdom and guidance. Pray for your leaders and for your fellow group members. Don't worry if it's a small gathering at first. Just be consistent with your desire to watch God work in your youth group.

I know a girl who was in a situation similar to yours. She did the things I've suggested here and soon others caught her vision. Today, her youth group is one of the largest in the United States. More importantly, students in the group are growing in their faith. A theologian named D.L. Moody said something like this: "The world has yet to see what one man or woman can do for the Lord if they are totally committed to God." God can do amazing things with your youth group, and he can start with you.

88. She's Ruining My Youth Group!

My cousin has been bringing a non-Christian friend to our youth group. She's really rude and insulting. She plays around during the Bible studies, and is totally distracting. I know God's mercy is for everyone, but I feel so angry at this girl, I don't even want her to come to the group. I know my feelings are wrong, but I don't know what to do. Any suggestions?

I can sure understand where you're coming from. It can be frustrating to be around someone who acts like a pain in the neck. But I also can't think of a better place for your cousin's non-Christian friend to be than at the youth group.

Who knows why she's acting the way she is. It may be that she's nervous in this new, foreign setting. She may not really understand that some of her behavior is inappropriate. Or she may just want to see what she can get away with. Hopefully, your youth leaders and your cousin will help her learn the boundaries of behavior. At the same time, the group needs to show her patience and respect, so she'll continue to feel welcome, despite her behavior.

If her behavior continues to bother you, talk to your youth pastor. He or she might not be aware of the effect this new girl is having on others. Or your youth pastor may be able to give you suggestions on specific ways you can help your cousin's friend feel more comfortable.

Your situation reminds me of Jesus' disciple, Peter. Before Jesus came along, Peter, or "Simon" as he was named then, was just a bigmouthed fisherman. But Jesus looked at this ill-mannered man and saw his potential. Peter became a leader of the early church because Jesus believed he could change. My prayer is that your cousin's non-Christian friend will one day use her energy and spunk for Jesus Christ. So pray for her and be patient with her. You never know what God has in store.

89. I Don't Want the Youth Group to Change

I belong to a wonderful youth group with intense worship and prayer time. But lately, a lot of non-Christians have been coming. And they're becoming the majority! I should feel glad, but they goof off during prayer time, and they don't care about God. How can my youth group go back to the way it was?

You actually have a good problem. Most youth groups struggle with worship and they definitely wish they had more non-Christians coming to their meetings. I don't think your youth group should go back to the way it was. This doesn't mean it won't take time for some of the non-Christians to get used to the way you worship, pray and generally "do" youth group. These students have probably spent little or no time in church. When they find themselves in a place like your youth group, it must seem very strange to them. Even so, there's obviously something that's attracting them to your group. It may be the friendship and love that's radiated, or maybe they've realized something is missing in their lives. Your group might be just the place for them to find the missing piece. Be patient with these non-Christians.

In fact, you may be about to experience revival in your youth group. Right before a great outpouring of the Spirit of God, there is often a wonderful time of worship and prayer from the believers. Don't expect the new believers or non-Christians to have the same fervor you and your friends have toward spiritual things. At the same time, make sure you have a solid place in your schedule to worship and pray. Share your concerns with your youth workers and student leaders. If the youth group is changing so dramatically, you may need to find another time for your leadership to come together for prayer and fellowship. Be sure to spend time in prayer for all the non-believers that are attending. It's also important to set aside some time to reach out to students who have never had the privilege of developing a personal relationship with God. This could involve spending time with them outside of school and youth group.

Remember, you never know what God has planned for your youth group. It sounds like he's preparing to do great things.

90. My Youth Director's Behavior Is Inappropriate

Our youth director is young, married and incredibly good-looking. But he's making a lot of people in our youth group very uncomfortable. He's always hugging the girls. He dresses in a sexy way, wearing cutoff T-shirts and ripped jeans with his underwear showing. I'm afraid to be alone with him. And the guys in our group think he's way too competitive in games. They say he's rough and gets really mad when he loses.

My mom talked to him about his behavior, but he laughed off her concerns, saying girls always fantasize about their youth directors. The church committee that works with him just lets him do what he wants. Even worse, the senior pastor is his uncle, so he probably wouldn't do anything either. Most of us love our youth group, but our youth leader is making it miserable. What can we do?

I believe youth workers have one of God's most important callings. Most of them are committed to sharing God's love with students. But as with any profession, there are a few youth workers who are misguided when it comes to lifestyle choices and appropriate behavior. It's clear your youth director must be confronted with these issues. Even if just one young woman feels uncomfortable with him, or if only a couple of the guys say he is too rough and competitive, it's time to get the issues on the table and talk. It sounds like you've tried to do just that. I want to encourage you to keep trying, for the good of everyone involved.

I suggest you use the Bible's model for handling conflict, Matthew 18:15-17.

Write down all the information you know to be fact. Leave

out any rumors and anything you can't back up as absolute truth. Talk over this list with your mom, or the adult you plan to take with you in step two.

Ask your mother or another friend and her parent to go with you to talk to your youth director privately. Confront him with the facts you've gathered. To "confront" doesn't mean to be negative or critical, but rather tell him in a caring way that you have some concerns about the youth group. If he listens to your concerns and makes some changes in his behavior, stop there and be thankful you've helped.

If he doesn't take you seriously, bring your concerns to the leadership of your church. This could be a meeting with the pastor, the committee you mentioned or other leaders in your congregation. Don't assume you know how they will respond. They most likely want what's best for the church and will listen seriously to your concerns. Again, stick with the facts. Ask the leadership to hear you, to pray about the next move and to inform you of what actions they plan to take. Hopefully, your youth director will listen to the leadership and make the necessary changes.

If nothing changes, you have some difficult decisions to make. The youth group members and their parents could call for a church meeting. You could make an appointment with a representative from your denomination. (The church office can help you find out who that is). Or you can consider worshiping in another church. These are all very serious steps and I hope you don't have to take the problem this far.

Your efforts to resolve the problems with your youth director may be just as important for his growth as they are for the group. Remember to pray for him and share your concerns in true Christian love.

91. I Want to Go to a Different Church

I don't like the new pastor at my church. He has said some very offensive things to my sister, and he seems like a hypocrite. My parents think very highly of this man and don't understand why I'm starting to hate church. I'd like to find a church where the pastor is a spiritual leader for me. But how can I tell my parents I want to change churches without hurting their feelings or making them mad?

Several years ago, I went to a church where the pastor was unfaithful to his wife and his commitment to Christ. He bothered me so much, that I soon went from being a joyful, active Christian to a bitter, resentful Christian. I was focused on a man and not the Lord. I'd hate to see the same thing happen to you.

On rare occasions it is probably right to leave a church when you can't respect your pastor. However, I would first challenge you to stay at your church and try and work through this problem.

The Bible calls the church the "body of Christ." Despite the fact that the church has some problems, we're still called to be committed to this body of Christ. Since our commitment and relationship with the church is so important to our spiritual life, I suggest you tell your parents how you feel about the pastor and your reasons for wanting to leave your church. Write out your thoughts and feelings ahead of time. Be as straightforward as possible and avoid exaggeration or gossip. Then set up a time when you and your parents can discuss this issue. Tell them you are seeking their advice and that you want them to listen to your feelings. And listen to what they have to say about the situation. Yes, you may hurt their feelings and, who knows, you may make them a little mad. But your relationship to the church of Christ is more important than a minor conflict with your parents that will pass.

Finally, I think you, as a family, should pray about your concerns. When facing a conflict, the easiest thing to do is to walk away. But the best method is to try and work through the conflict.

92. How Can I Find a Church?

I'm sixteen and have never been to church except to visit. I want to get involved in a fun youth group and start going to church. How do I find a church I'll like?

Churches can feel pretty intimidating when you don't know anyone and you're not sure about all the "rules and rituals" of the place. That's why I want to encourage you to talk to your Christian friends.

Even if you don't have a lot of close Christian friends, there are probably other Christians at your school. Visit a prayer group or other fellowship group at your school. Ask some of those students about their churches. Tell them you'd like to join an active youth group. I bet most of them will be happy to tell you about the youth groups they attend. Don't be shy about asking if you can visit their churches and youth groups.

I'd encourage you to check out both the youth group and the regular service at the churches you visit. When you go to a youth group, ask yourself a few questions: *Does the youth group get along well? Do I feel like this group can help me grow spiritually?*

Do the adult leaders seem like people I could talk to easily? And when you attend a church service, ask yourself: *Can I feel God's presence during the service? Do I understand the pastor's sermon? Is God's Word a central part of the service?* Visit a few churches to get a feel for what you like and don't like in a church. And keep in mind that no church this side of heaven is perfect. Pick the church that will help you grow in your Christian faith and one where, frankly, you will like the people and the atmosphere.

While being part of a fun youth group is a great reason to go to church, I hope you'll keep in mind that church is about a lot more than fun and fellowship.

The word "church" actually can mean two things. It can mean the building with the steeple where people go to worship. But "church" also refers to what the Bible calls the "body of Christ," which is made up of all Christians around the world. Even though Jesus Christ is not walking the earth in the flesh, the world sees Jesus Christ through God's people, the church. Demonstrating God's love to the world is a big job, one that no Christian can do alone. That's why we need to be part of the body by plugging in to a church.

Church also helps our own faith grow. Just like a plant can't grow without sun and water, a Christian seldom grows without the fellowship of a church body.

Choosing a church home may be one of the most important decisions of your life, and I'm glad you're taking it seriously. Your faith will grow in a big way because of this decision.

93. I Want More Out of Church

I go to church every week, but I don't get much out of it. I have a hard time paying attention and my mind wanders a lot. There aren't many people my age in the church, so we don't have a youth group or anything. How can I get more out of church?

You're not the only one who sometimes finds it tough to pay attention in church. There are times during church when my mind slips away to far-off places. Other times I don't feel like I'm on the same wavelength as our pastor, making it harder to get much out of the sermon.

The way I look at it, my attitude about church has the biggest impact on how I feel about being there. If I come to the service ready for worship, I have a much better experience than when I come with a negative attitude. I try to remember that church is not about being entertained for an hour or two on Sunday morning. It's about coming together with other Christians to worship our incredible God. This means what I put into church is perhaps more important than what I get out of church.

There are several things you can do to prepare yourself for worship. Stop by or call the church office each week and ask about that week's sermon topic. Ask which Bible verses will be used in the service. Take some time before you actually get to church to look over these verses so they're familiar to you when they're read. During the service itself, focus on God, using the service to guide your thoughts. Think about the ways God has worked in your life during the past week. Use the time you're in church to praise God for these things. And think about ways you can actually be involved in the worship service. You could sing in the choir, or offer to read a Scripture passage. If you like working with children, volunteer to help teach a Sunday school class. These things will help you meet more people and feel more involved in the life of the church.

Regardless of how we feel about going to church, the Bible is clear that worshiping God together is an essential part of every Christian's life. Hebrews 10:25 says, "Let us not give up meeting together, as some are in the habit of doing, but let us encourage one another."

It's hard to find the kind of fellowship the Bible talks about when you don't have many peers in the church. Since there is no youth group at your church, you might want to think about joining a Christian club at your high school, or becoming involved with another church's youth group. That way, you can still be part of your own church, and find the fellowship you're looking for. And don't forget, it doesn't take a large group to have a Bible study or plan a few fun activities. I encourage you to get together with the other people at your church who are your age. They may be feeling the same way you do and would love to have some friends at church. You may have to work a little to find the right kind of group for you, but the fellowship will be well worth the effort.

94. How Do I Start a Youth Group?

I'm trying to get a youth group started at my new church. The problem is, there aren't really any youth. I used to go to a different church, where there was a good-sized group, and I really enjoyed it.

Recently, I've been inviting people from my school to church, but it's not having much effect. Do you have any tips?

Congratulations! You have the opportunity to pioneer youth ministry at your church. Renewal and revival in a church often begins when students get serious about prayer and then take on the leadership needed to begin a work.

I don't think there are any magic formulas, but here are some suggestions:

Pray. Every movement of God begins with prayer. Pray daily and often. And be sure to find one other person to pray with.

Start small. Don't worry if only a few are involved. Five, three, or even two students are more than you have now. A small group has the ability to build close relationships that will help you grow spiritually.

Find adult help. There must be someone in your church who's willing to give a new youth group some time and attention. Recruit people you think would be a positive influence in your life and the lives of your friends. Ask that person to help you find the right resources to lead a Bible study or a youth group meeting.

Invite friends. You say you've been asking friends to church. Keep asking! Youth ministry experts tell us that one out of four students who are invited to a youth group meeting will attend.

Maybe God brought you to this church for a special reason.

It would be just like God to use a student like you to help start a spiritual movement in your church and school.

95. I Don't Get the Trinity

Why do we call God "Father"? And what role does the Father have in our lives that's different from Jesus and the Holy Spirit?

To answer your first question, we call God "Father" because Jesus said to. He instructed his disciples to pray to "Abba" (Mt 6:5-15), which means "Daddy" in the English language. Never before had God, the almighty Creator of the universe, been addressed so personally and informally in prayer. With just one word, Jesus showed that God is our loving Father, and we are his children.

Now about the role of the Father. Your question deals with one of the great doctrines of Christianity called the Trinity. Although it's a very difficult idea to grasp, we believe in one God in three persons: the Father, the Son (Jesus) and the Holy Spirit. Each person of the Trinity has a distinct role. Generally speaking, God the Father is the Creator, Jesus is our Savior and the Holy Spirit lives in each Christian, comforting, empowering and leading. But even that's an oversimplification; in reality, the roles are shared by all three persons of the Trinity. The Trinity is a complex concept, and even the world's top theologians have difficulty defining the roles of all three persons.

But it's not important to have the Trinity all figured out. What's important is worshiping and loving the great God the Trinity represents.

96. What's the Unforgivable Sin?

What is the "sin against the Holy Spirit"? Is it something I could have done in my past—something I didn't know about? I'm worried I might go to hell.

Let me put your fears at ease: You haven't committed the "sin against the Holy Spirit," also known as the "unforgivable sin."

When people talk about the unforgivable sin, they're usually referring to statements Jesus makes in the Gospels of Matthew and Mark. Jesus says in Mark 3:28-29, "I tell you the truth, all the sins and blasphemies of men will be forgiven them. But whoever blasphemes against the Holy Spirit will never be forgiven; he is guilty of an eternal sin."

I admit, Jesus' words sound confusing and incredibly harsh. But realize that Jesus talked about this sin right after the Pharisees had seen the healing power of God and called it the work of the devil. They not only rejected Jesus, they said he was possessed by a demon! In powerful words, Jesus condemned them for such complete disbelief.

But the wonderful thing about having a relationship with Jesus is you cannot commit the unforgivable sin. There is no sin too big for God to forgive! When you became a Christian, you believed in Christ's death on the cross for your sins and acknowledged your need for God's forgiveness. You entered into eternal life and an eternal relationship with God. Jesus Christ has paid for *all* your sins—past failures, present struggles and future faults. Romans 8:1 puts it this way: "Therefore, there is now no condemnation for those who are in Christ Jesus." No sin will ever separate you from your loving heavenly Father.

97. Isn't Everyone a Part of a Cult?

I belong to the Church of Jesus Christ of Latter-day Saints (Mormon Church). I heard someone call Mormonism a cult. When I looked up cult in the dictionary it says that a cult is a group that follows a leader. Catholics follow the pope, Lutherans follow Martin Luther and Mormons follow the teachings of Christ from the Bible and the Book of Mormon. Doesn't this make everyone part of a cult then?

If you're looking at the Webster's dictionary definition of "cult," you are absolutely right. A cult in its simplest meaning is a system of religious worship. But to Christians, a cult is a religious group with beliefs outside the mainstream teaching of the Christian faith. I have very good friends who are Mormon. We have a wonderful common bond in similar family values and other issues surrounding our lives. However, we must agree that the Mormon church and mainstream Christianity are quite different on a few key points.

Here are two points to ponder:

1. Joseph Smith: Was he a prophet or not? Did God send the angel Moroni to deliver the Book of Mormon to Joseph Smith, as Mormons claim? Obviously, Mormons believe that Joseph Smith was a prophet and that the Book of Mormon is a holy book. Christians do not believe Smith was a prophet or that the Book of Mormon is holy. Christians believe the Bible—and nothing else—is the only true Word of God. Mormons believe they have a "new scripture," sort of a 19th-century addition to the Bible. That's a major difference in our faith and practices.

2. One of the other major differences is salvation. Mormons believe salvation (going to heaven) comes through good works and that all people will spend eternity on some level of a multistoried heaven. The level will be determined by the scope of each person's good works. The Christian view is radically different. We believe that salvation is a free gift of God's grace for all who believe and accept Jesus Christ into their life (see Eph 2:8-9; Jn 14:1-6).

There are several other major differences between Mormonism and Christianity such as our view of God, the Bible and sin. So it is very safe to say the teaching of the Christian faith and Mormonism are different at some of our core beliefs.

For more information about why Christians believe Mormonism is a cult, read *The God Makers* by Ed Decker (Harvest House) or *What's with the Dudes at the Door?* by Kevin Johnson and James White (Bethany House).

98. Will God Forgive Suicide?

I heard that if you're a Christian and commit suicide, you go to hell. Surely God knows how much hurt you've been through, so why would he send you to hell?

Whenever a church or youth group has a Bible study or discussion on the subject of suicide, the first question seems to be about hell. At one time a major Christian denomination taught that if a person committed suicide, they would be sent straight to hell. This denomination has since backed off of that thinking, but the idea is still on the minds of many.

The Bible is very specific on several important subjects. Where it is specific we are called simply to believe. It is specific and clear, for instance, on heaven and hell—not how they relate to suicide but rather to our relationship with Jesus Christ. Romans 10:9-10 says, "That if you confess with your mouth, 'Jesus is Lord,' and believe in your heart that God raised him from the dead, you will be saved. For it is with your heart that you believe and are justified, and it is with your mouth that you confess and are saved." It is clear that our salvation depends on our relationship with God, not on a specific action.

Again, and as mentioned above, the Bible is not clear on the subject of suicide. Nevertheless, I strongly believe it is never God's will for someone to commit suicide. For a person contemplating suicide, the issue is not hell, but finding the hope to get past their pain and live the abundant life Christ offers. God doesn't promise a life free of pain, but he does offer to never leave us nor forsake us (see Dt 31:8). When a person attempts suicide they have basically lost all hope. But Christ is a restorer of hope.

If you or a friend is considering suicide, I strongly urge you to tell a trusted adult—a parent, a teacher, a pastor—right away. They'll point you or your friend to the help that is needed. Or call one of the following numbers: 9-1-1, 1-800-SUICIDE, 1-800-NEW-LIFE or 1-800-383-HOPE.

99. Can You Be Saved After Death?

My friends and I have a hard question we can't find the answer to. Can someone get saved after they die or go to hell? What does the Bible say?

It would be nice if there were an opportunity to change your mind in hell, but the Bible gives no indication that this will be possible. Hebrews 9:27 says we are all "destined to die once, and after that to face judgment."

Another passage that seems to shut the door to a "second chance" is a parable Jesus told in Luke 16:19-31. The parable is about a rich man who died and went to hell. In his agony, the rich man looked up to heaven and cried out for mercy. In response to his cries, the man was told a chasm separated heaven and hell—a chasm that could never be crossed.

As hard as it is to hear, eternal separation from God is the punishment for people who don't accept Christ as Lord and Savior. But please understand that it's not God's desire for anyone to spend eternity in hell. As it says in 2 Peter 3:9, "He is patient with you, not wanting anyone to perish, but everyone to come to repentance."

So my encouragement to you is to concentrate on the present. I can't tell you what will happen between death and judgment, but I can tell you that God desires for each one of us to experience his love and grace right here, right now.

100. Wearing Makeup

I go to a very conservative church, where women can't wear makeup or jewelry. I just don't think it's wrong to wear this stuff. My dad and I are getting into arguments about it. I've tried to show him from the Bible why I'm right, but he always seems to find a different verse to contradict me. What should I do about this situation?

You may be doing all you can, for now. Keep talking with your dad and other leaders in the church. Learn everything you can from the Bible about these issues and make sure you don't get bitter at God over your dad's opinions.

The easiest thing to do is rebel or do things behind your dad's back. But the right way is to look at this as a season in your life that will one day change. Ask God for wisdom and guidance, and when you're an adult you can make whatever decision you believe is God's will for you.

I know some very wonderful people who have come from conservative churches like yours. The individuals who have a vibrant faith are the ones who chose their battles carefully and focused on a positive, loving, grace-filled relationship with God.

101. Is Dancing a Sin?

The church I go to believes dancing is wrong. That hasn't been a big deal to me until this year. I'm a junior, and we have the Junior Ball coming up. I know there will be dancing there, but I really want to go. What should I do?

What you end up doing—whether you go to the dance or not—isn't as important as the questions you work through to reach your decision. The questions you're probably already asking yourself are, "Why is dancing wrong?" and "If I go to the ball, what will people at my church say?"

Now is the best time to begin taking ownership of your beliefs. But you should also get together with your parents and your youth leader or pastor to discuss this further. Is your church really dead set against dancing, or only certain kinds of dancing? What is the biblical basis for this belief? See if they might have some practical guidelines for you if you go to the ball. And ask them, "What advice would you give me in seeking God's direction in dancing and other cultural issues?"

You might be pleasantly surprised by what you hear. On the other hand, you may find your parents also have reservations about dancing. If they're not open to further discussion, I think you should respect their wishes by planning an alternate event or staying home.

Let's say you don't get a strong response either way. This is your chance to ask God for wisdom as you make a decision. Keep James 1:5 in mind: "If any of you lacks wisdom, he should ask God, who gives generously to all without finding fault, and it will be given to him."

102. What's Wrong With Yoga?

My aunt practices Yoga. I don't know much about it, so I've looked at some Christian Web sites to see what they say. I haven't found much. What should a Christian's perspective be about Yoga?

I can't say there's an official "Christian perspective" on this issue. Some Christians have no objections to the practice of Yoga. In fact, there are even churches that offer Yoga as a part of their exercise programs. But I have a few concerns about being involved with this activity.

While Yoga produces notable health benefits, for some it's more than an exercise program, it's a way of life. Yoga actually means "yoke" or "union." Followers of the Yoga way of life would say it's a union between the personal aspects of ourselves and the "divine presence."

Some Christians have told me that Yoga makes them feel closer to Jesus, in addition to making their body and mind feel better. I think what they're saying is possible, but they aren't practicing true Yoga. True Yoga, from a spiritual level, has its roots in other religions besides Christianity. Most practitioners of Yoga regard the *Yoga Sutras of Patanjali* as the most important handbook on the subject. The other text on Yoga is the Hindu scripture, the *Bhagavad Gita*. A look into these texts will reveal the "divine" as an impersonal, formless energy that somehow guides the universe. Therefore, an alignment with the "divine presence" is not an encounter with Jesus.

I'm not sure if your aunt recognizes Yoga's spiritual aspects. But knowing Yoga's roots in Eastern Mysticism, I would encourage her to search elsewhere for the benefits she finds in Yoga—specifically through her relationship with Christ, prayer and a meaningful exercise program. A balanced life focusing on our spiritual, mental, social and physical development is a very important part of living a meaningful life.

103. Is Hypnotism Satanic?

A hypnotist came to our school for an assembly. He said hypnotism was the ability to open your mind in order to use it to full capacity. He was very convincing. But when I told my pastor about it, he said hypnotism is satanic and that it clears your mind to let demons in. Now I don't know what to think. Does the Bible say anything about hypnotism? Is it really satanic?

Hypnotism can be very frightening when used to go against what the Lord wants in our lives. I believe, like your pastor, that many use hypnotism in an unchristian manner. Often when people use hypnotism, it's probably not for the reason of glorifying Jesus Christ.

Some Christian leaders in the field of counseling would say that hypnotism from a Christian therapist can be helpful in some cases. I know of a woman who had been abused, and her Christian therapist used hypnotism to help in her healing process.

I also know people who've quit smoking with the help of hypnotism. However, I would caution you and anyone reading this answer to refrain from playing around with hypnotism.

I'm not sure about the connection between "demons" and hypnotism, but many who practice the occult also practice hypnotism. Unfortunately, Satan is very active, and there's nothing he would like better than to keep our focus off our relationship with Jesus Christ. The Bible speaks of an unseen spiritual realm with both evil and good and I believe we should never dabble in this spirit world when we don't know what we're doing.

You were wise to seek the wisdom of your pastor. You can also ask yourself a few questions to clear up any confusion you might still have: Does this experience glorify Jesus Christ? Do I have any doubts that this experience may not be from God? Have I prayed about this? If you're still confused and concerned about this subject, ask your pastor to help you find another Christian you could talk with who has studied it in depth.